# The Growth and Influence of Islam

## IN THE NATIONS OF ASIA AND CENTRAL ASIA

# Kyrgyzstan

# The Growth and Influence of Islam

## IN THE NATIONS OF ASIA AND CENTRAL ASIA

Afghanistan

Azerbaijan

Bangladesh

Indonesia

Islam in Asia: Facts and Figures

Islamist Terrorism in Asia

Kazakhstan

The Kurds

Kyrgyzstan

Malaysia

Muslims in China

Muslims in India

Muslims in Russia

Pakistan

Tajikistan

Turkmenistan

Uzbekistan

# The Growth and Influence of Islam
## IN THE NATIONS OF ASIA AND CENTRAL ASIA

# Kyrgyzstan

## Daniel E. Harmon

Mason Crest Publishers
Philadelphia

Produced by OTTN Publishing, Stockton, New Jersey

**Mason Crest Publishers**
370 Reed Road
Broomall, PA 19008
www.masoncrest.com

3  5  7  9  8  6  4  2

Library of Congress Cataloging-in-Publication Data

Harmon, Daniel E.
  Kyrgyzstan / Daniel E. Harmon.
     p. cm. — (Growth and influence of Islam in the nations of Asia and Central Asia)
  Includes bibliographical references and index.
  ISBN 1-59084-883-7
  1. Kyrgyzstan—Juvenile literature.  I. Title. II. Series.
  DK913.H37 2005
  958.43—dc22
                              2004019827

# Table of Contents

Introduction.................................................7
  Harvey Sicherman, the Foreign Policy Research Institute

Place in the World.....................................13

The Land ..................................................21

The History..............................................33

The Economy, Politics, and Religion ...................51

The People ...............................................69

Cities and Communities ...............................87

Foreign Relations.......................................97

Chronology .............................................110

Glossary ...............................................112

Further Reading........................................113

Internet Resources.....................................114

Index ...................................................115

**Dr. Harvey Sicherman, president and director of the Foreign Policy Research Institute, is the author of such books as *America the Vulnerable: Our Military Problems and How to Fix Them* (2002) and *Palestinian Autonomy, Self-Government and Peace* (1993).**

# Introduction

## by Dr. Harvey Sicherman

America's triumph in the Cold War promised a new burst of peace and prosperity. Indeed, the decade between the demise of the Soviet Union and the destruction of September 11, 2001, proved deceptively hopeful. Today, of course, we are more fully aware—to our sorrow—of the dangers and troubles no longer just below the surface.

The Muslim identities of most of the terrorists at war with the United States have also provoked great interest in Islam as well as the role of religion in politics. It is crucial for Americans not to assume that Osama bin Laden's ideas are identical to those of most Muslims or, for that matter, that most Muslims are Arabs. A truly world religion, Islam claims hundreds of millions of adherents, from every ethnic group scattered across the globe. This book series covers the growth and influence of Muslims in Asia and Central Asia.

A glance at the map establishes the extraordinary coverage of our authors. Every climate and terrain may be found, along with every form of human society, from the nomadic groups of the Central Asian steppes to highly sophisticated cities such as Singapore, New Delhi, and Shanghai. The economies of the nations examined in this series are likewise highly diverse. In some, barter systems are still used; others incorporate modern stock markets. In some of the countries, large oil reserves hold out the prospect of prosperity. Other countries, such as India and China, have progressed by moving from a government-controlled to a more market-based economic system. Still other countries have built wealth on service and shipping.

Central Asia and Asia is a heavily armed and turbulent area. Three of its states (China, India, and Pakistan) are nuclear powers, and one (Kazakhstan) only recently rid itself of nuclear weapons. But it is also a place where the horse and mule remain indispensable instruments of war. All of the region's states have an extensive history of conflict, domestic and international, old and new. Afghanistan, for example, has known little but invasion and civil war over the past two decades.

Governments include dictatorships, democracies, and hybrids without a name; centralized and decentralized administrations; and older patterns of tribal and clan associations. The region is a veritable encyclopedia of political expression.

Although such variety defies easy generalities, it is still possible to make several observations. First, the geopolitics of Central Asia and Asia reflect the impact of empires and the struggles of post-imperial independence. Central Asia, a historic corridor for traders and soldiers, was the scene of Russian expansion well into Soviet times. While Kazakhstan's leaders participated in the historic meeting of December 25, 1991, that dissolved the Soviet Union, the rest of the region's newly independent republics hardly expected it. They have found it difficult to grapple with a sometimes tenuous independence, buffeted by a strong residual Russian influence, the absence of settled institutions, the temptation of newly valuable natural resources, and mixed populations lacking a solid national identity. The shards of the Soviet Union have often been sharp—witness the Russian war in Chechnya—and sometimes fatal for those ambitious to grasp them.

**Young ethnic Kyrgyz children wear traditional clothing at a festival celebrating their country's heritage.**

Moving further east, one encounters an older devolution, that of the half-century since the British Raj dissolved into India and Pakistan (the latter giving violent birth to Bangladesh in 1971). Only recently, partly under the impact of the war on terrorism, have these nuclear-armed neighbors and adversaries found it possible to renew attempts at reconciliation. Still further east, Malaysia shares a British experience, but Indonesia has been influenced by its Dutch heritage. Even China defines its own borders along the lines of the Qing empire (the last pre-republican dynasty) at its most expansionist (including Tibet and Taiwan). These imperial histories lie heavily upon the politics of the region.

A second aspect worth noting is the variety of economic experimentation afoot in the area. State-dominated economic strategies, still in the ascendant, are separating government from the actual running of commerce and industry. "Privatization," however, is frequently a byword for crony capitalism and corruption. Yet in dynamic economies such as that of China, as well as an increasingly productive India, hundreds of millions of people have dramatically improved both their standard of living and their hope for the future. All of them aspire to benefit from international trade. Competitive advantages, such as low-cost labor (in some cases trained in high technology) and valuable natural resources (oil, gas, and minerals), promise much. This is indeed a revolution of rising expectations, some of which are being satisfied.

Yet more than corruption threatens this progress. Population increase, even though moderating, still overwhelms educational and employment opportunities. Many countries are marked by extremes of wealth and poverty, especially between rural and urban areas. Dangerous jealousies threaten ethnic groups (such as anti-Chinese violence in Indonesia).

**This rare color photograph from 1905 shows a family of Kyrgyz nomads on the Central Asian steppe.**

Hopelessly overburdened public services portend turmoil. Public health, never adequate, is harmed further by environmental damage to critical resources (such as the Aral Sea). By and large, Central Asian and Asian countries are living well beyond their infrastructures.

Third and finally, Islam has deeply affected the states and peoples of the region. Indonesia is the largest Muslim state in the world, and India hosts the second-largest Muslim population. Islam is not only the official religion of many states, it is the very reason for Pakistan's existence. But Islamic practices and groups vary: the well-known Sunni and Shiite groups are joined by energetic Salafi (Wahabi) and Sufi movements. Over the last 20 years especially, South and Central Asia have become battle-grounds for competing Shiite (Iranian) and Wahabi (Saudi) doctrines, well financed from abroad and aggressively antagonistic toward non-Muslims and each other. Resistance to the Soviet invasion of Afghanistan brought these groups battle-tested warriors and organizers. The war on terrorism has exposed just how far-reaching and active the new advocates of holy war (jihad) can be. Indonesia, in particular, is the scene of rivalry between an older, tolerant Islam and the jihadists. But Pakistan also faces an Islamic identity crisis. And India, wracked by sectarian strife, must hold together its democratic framework despite Muslim and Hindu extremists. This newly significant struggle within Islam, superimposed on an older Muslim history, will shape political and economic destinies throughout the region and beyond. Hence, the focus of our series.

We hope that these books will enlighten both teacher and student about a critical subject in a critical area of the world. Central Asia and Asia would be important in their own right to Americans; arguably, after 9/11, they became vital to our national security. And the enduring impact of Islam is a crucial factor we must understand. We at the Foreign Policy Research Institute hope these books will illuminate both the facts and the prospects.

A sculpture of the ancient hero Manas, who is revered by the Kyrgyz people. The hero of the world's longest epic poem, Manas united the Kyrgyz tribes a thousand years ago and inspired generations of storytellers.

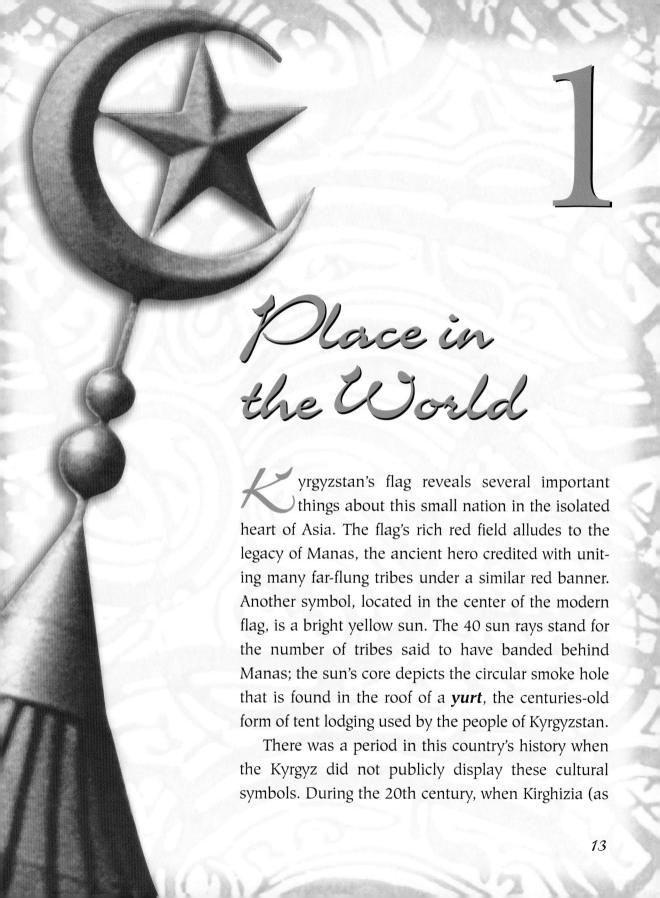

# 1

# Place in the World

Kyrgyzstan's flag reveals several important things about this small nation in the isolated heart of Asia. The flag's rich red field alludes to the legacy of Manas, the ancient hero credited with uniting many far-flung tribes under a similar red banner. Another symbol, located in the center of the modern flag, is a bright yellow sun. The 40 sun rays stand for the number of tribes said to have banded behind Manas; the sun's core depicts the circular smoke hole that is found in the roof of a **yurt**, the centuries-old form of tent lodging used by the people of Kyrgyzstan.

There was a period in this country's history when the Kyrgyz did not publicly display these cultural symbols. During the 20th century, when Kirghizia (as it was then known) was a republic of the Soviet Union and forced to follow the principles of the U.S.S.R.'s Communist regime, the people were discouraged from honoring Manas in their folk songs and poems. Today the Kyrgyz remember their hero openly; even the country's international airport, located near the capital city of Bishkek, bears Manas's name. In fact, in the regional language the word *Kyrgyz* means "40 clans," referring to the union that Manas achieved. Even Kyrgyz of other ethnic backgrounds are well versed in the Manas saga.

The people also are proud of their traditional ***nomadic*** lifestyle. The yurt was the only kind of home their ancestors knew. Most Kyrgyz today are settled in permanent housing, but many rural families still dwell in portable yurts during the season when they take their herds to find pastures in the mountains.

**A Kyrgyz family outside their yurt, or circular tent; the father is chopping wood for cooking. Nomadic rituals and traditions are still a source of pride for many people of Kyrgyzstan.**

Kyrgyzstan's flag and its symbols are a source of pride, but they also illustrate a dilemma the country faces today: the allegiance to family, tribe, and ethnic heritage is stronger than to a united republic. As the Kyrgyz adjust to their newly won independence, the challenge they face is to remain united as they adjust to a new political system and deal with limited natural resources. Time-honored ways may still be preferred in Kyrgyzstan, but there is no denying that the people have experienced dramatic changes in recent years.

## Roaming Inhabitants, Conquerors, and Travelers

Kyrgyzstan is located in Central Asia, an obscure region little known to most outsiders. It is part of what has been called "inner Asia," because the countries in this part of the great Asian continent are far removed from the nearest oceans. Despite the obscurity of its location, the area that is now Kyrgyzstan has been a place of strategic importance since ancient times. It also has been the site of a curious interaction among diverse peoples from the far west and east. A changing cast of residents, who over time migrated in and out of the region, has included wandering clans of herders as well as settled farmers. People of past eras were subdued by powerful armies from the Middle East, Mongolia, and Russia.

As the 20th century ended, the people of the newly formed Kyrgyz Republic were for the first time responsible for their own government. Some question whether they are better off or worse off as an independent country. As the issue remains open to debate, numerous foreign powers continue to seek influence in the region.

## A Confusing Identity

The Kyrgyz Republic, or as it is known to natives, Kyrgyz Respublikasy, has had its name spelled in countless ways. Before independence in 1991, it was known variously to outsiders as Kirghizia, Kirgizia, Kirgiziya, and Kirgizistan. As a Soviet territory during the 20th century, it was called the Kirgiz (or Kirghiz) Soviet Socialist Republic. Even today, observers and writers use Kyrgyzstan, Kyrghyzstan, Kirghistan, and Kirgizia. This book will use modern standard spellings, referring to the country as Kyrgyzstan, its general populace as Kyrgyzstanis, and members of the ethnic group as Kyrgyz. Earlier spelling variations will be used when appropriate.

Kyrgyzstan's neighbors are Kazakhstan in the north, China in the east and southeast, Tajikistan in the southwest, and Uzbekistan in the west. In most places, mountain ridges form the country's international boundary lines.

Central Asia is the south-central part of the former Soviet Union, comprised of Kyrgyzstan and four other former Soviet republics: Kazakhstan (the largest), Tajikistan, Turkmenistan, and Uzbekistan. Kyrgyzstan is the second smallest of these five countries, encompassing 76,641 square miles (199,267 square kilometers). The Central Asian republics were among the poorest in the Soviet Union. Most of their ethnic peoples, including the Kyrgyz, belong to the Turkic language group. An exception is the Tajik, most of whom speak a variation of Farsi, the official language of Iran.

It is fairly common for westerners to make the mistake of using "Russia" and the "former Soviet Union" interchangeably. This error is founded on the notion that the two entities are one and the same country; in reality the Soviet Union, or the U.S.S.R., was a vast country consisting of 15 Soviet republics. Russia was the largest and most dominant of these very different republics.

Long before there was a Soviet Union, under the imperial rule of the tsars, Russia annexed the Central Asian territories during the late 1800s. After the Bolshevik Revolution of 1917 and the subsequent rise of the Communist Soviet state, the territories became part of the Soviet Union.

**In the village of Uch-Korgon in southwest Kyrgyzstan, an elderly ethnic Kyrgyz man walks past a Soviet-era memorial to soldiers who fell in the Second World War. Kyrgyzstan was part of the Soviet Union from the early 1920s until its breakup in 1991.**

During the era of Soviet prominence in the 20th century, outside observers commonly referred to the "Russian influence" or "Russification" in the Central Asian republics. Many of the newcomers who settled in Central Asia during the 19th and 20th centuries were of Russian nationality. (Kyrgyzstani citizens of Russian lineage, many of whom live in the industrialized northern cities, still constitute a sizeable percentage of the country's population. With the people of other eastern European countries, they make up the Slavic citizens of Kyrgyzstan.) However, in studying Kyrgyzstan, it is important to keep in mind the difference between the terms "Russian" and "Soviet." Russia's influence is indeed an element of Kyrgyzstan's history and society, but it was the higher Soviet government in Moscow—not the Russian republic's administration—that directly controlled much of Kyrygyzstan's affairs during the Soviet era.

## A Country With an Islamic Majority

In modern times, communism has been one of two overshadowing influences in Kyrgyzstan and the rest of Central Asia—the other has been Islam. During Soviet rule, the practice of Islam and other religions was repressed. With the breakup of the Soviet Union in 1991, outside observers wondered whether Islam would become the dominant factor in Central Asian politics. Most of the citizens of these republics, after all, are Muslims. Radical Muslim organizations in recent decades have vied for political power, and some have even used terrorist tactics. Some experts feared Kyrgyzstan and its neighbors would follow the path of nearby Iran, where a revolution in the late 1970s created a strict Islam-centered government.

To date, such a revolution has not happened. One significant factor is Kyrgyzstan's geography. The country's remote location and limited transportation system, which discourage foreign investors and traders, also tend to discourage the spread of radical ideology from the Middle East. Another reason, analysts of current affairs point out, is that most Central Asian Muslims lack the religious zeal that ignited the Iranian revolution. Islam did not spread to the northern parts of Kyrgyzstan until the 18th century—a relatively recent development in the long history of the region. In the modern era, the non-Muslim influences of Europe have continued to be prevalent in Central Asia.

Other issues complicate Kyrgyzstan's identity. For instance, the country's official language has been a matter of contention since the early Soviet era. The Soviets wanted Russian to be taught and mastered by all

**Kyrgyzstan's first elected president, Askar Akayev, wears a traditional *kalpak* headpiece; with him is the country's first lady, his wife Mayram Akayeva. Akayev served until April 2005, when he resigned following widespread protests.**

the people in the union, but just before independence Kyrgyzstan recognized Kyrgyz as the republic's official language. Then in 2001, the policy changed again, with the government establishing Russian as a second official language, of equal importance to Kyrgyz.

Kyrgyzstan shares issues of identity and national unity with other Central Asian countries. In addition, like its regional neighbors Kyrgyzstan has floundered economically since becoming independent. To revitalize its economy in the 21st century, the country is hard pressed to maintain a democratic government and a free market system.

**Wildflowers grow in the Tian Shan Mountains near Tokmak, Kyrgyzstan. Mountains and glaciers cover most of the country.**

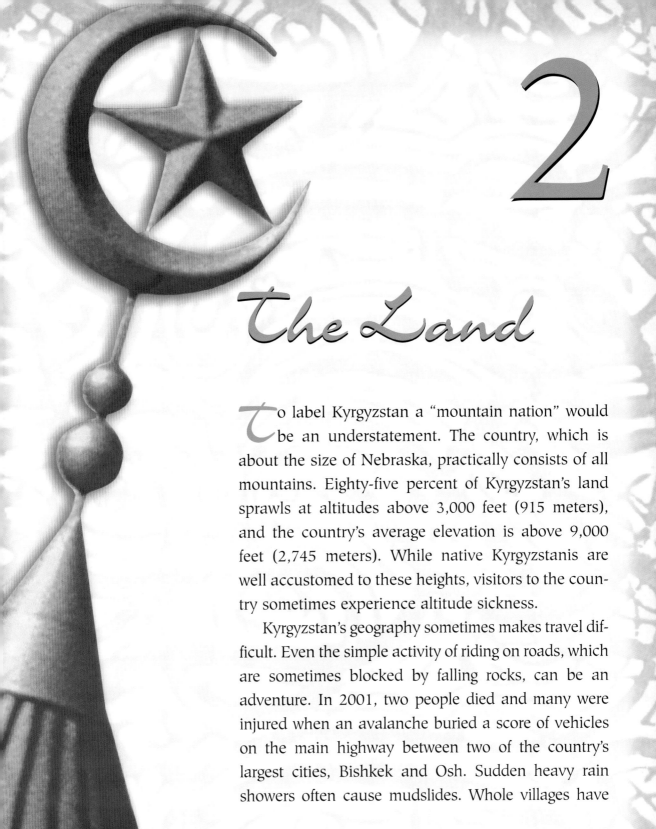

# 2

# The Land

To label Kyrgyzstan a "mountain nation" would be an understatement. The country, which is about the size of Nebraska, practically consists of all mountains. Eighty-five percent of Kyrgyzstan's land sprawls at altitudes above 3,000 feet (915 meters), and the country's average elevation is above 9,000 feet (2,745 meters). While native Kyrgyzstanis are well accustomed to these heights, visitors to the country sometimes experience altitude sickness.

Kyrgyzstan's geography sometimes makes travel difficult. Even the simple activity of riding on roads, which are sometimes blocked by falling rocks, can be an adventure. In 2001, two people died and many were injured when an avalanche buried a score of vehicles on the main highway between two of the country's largest cities, Bishkek and Osh. Sudden heavy rain showers often cause mudslides. Whole villages have been consumed by such disasters, which have become more common in modern times due to the erosion caused by poor forestry practices and excessive grazing.

## Celestial Mountains

The Tian Shan mountain range along China's northwestern border covers most of Kyrgyzstan. Tian Shan means "celestial," a reference to the heavenly appearance of the mountains' angular, towering slopes. A branch of the Tian Shan, the Alai mountain range, is located in the southwestern part of Kyrgyzstan. Also in the south are the Kok Shaal-Tau and At-Bashy ranges. The Chatkal Mountains lie to the northwest, above the Fergana Valley. Geologists refer to Kyrgyzstan's mountains as being "young," because they rise high and sharp, their peaks not yet blunted by time.

Some of the largest mountain glaciers on earth can be found in the Tian Shan system. Kyrgyzstan is known not so much for the size of its glaciers, though, as for their number—more than 6,000 can be found within the country's borders.

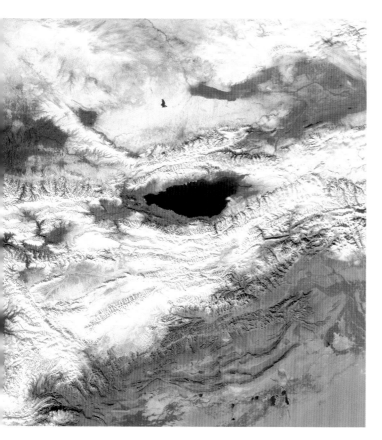

**The silvery snow appearing in this satellite image highlights the Tian Shan and Alai Mountains that dominate Kyrgyzstan. The large body of water between the mountains in eastern Kyrgyzstan is Lake Issyk-Kul, the world's second-largest alpine lake.**

Geologists calculate that altogether these glaciers contain about 23 trillion cubic feet (172 trillion gallons) of water. According to estimates, if all Kyrgyzstan's glaciers and snow were to melt, 9 feet (3 meters) of water would inundate the country's lowlands.

Lofty peaks and glaciers make Kyrgyzstan a place of awe-inspiring vistas. The tallest of the mountains is Pik Pobedy (Mount Victory), located on the Chinese border in the northeastern corner. More than 5 miles (7,439 meters) high, it is the second-tallest mountain in all the former Soviet republics. Another high peak, located on the Kazakhstan border, is Khan-Tengri. It is renowned internationally as a challenge for climbers. Many other mountains in the main Tian Shan system are higher than 15,000 feet (4,500 meters).

The high mountaintops of Kyrgyzstan are always covered with snow. In fact, as much as three-fourths of Kyrgyzstan's land area is covered year-round by glaciers or snow. Yet the mountainsides also offer natural grasslands that sustain a wide variety of animal life. Beside the herds of livestock that have supported nomads of the region for thousands of years, Kyrgyzstan is home to antelope, ibex, wolves, wild boars, bears, lynx, deer, mountain goats, snow leopards, and smaller creatures including pikas, hares, hedgehogs, gophers, and marmots. Eagles and other birds of prey, as well as countless smaller bird species, also inhabit the country.

Plant life includes colorful wildflowers and trees, notably spruce, juniper, and larch. The Tian Shan Mountains are famous for their white spruce. Many cherry, apricot, and apple orchards are found in the country, as is the largest natural-growth walnut forest in the world.

## A Country of Lakes and Rivers

Kyrgyzstan is a land of lakes, numbering about 2,000. Many are small and are set high amid the mountain ridges. The largest, Issyk-Kul, is one of the largest bodies of water in Central Asia, second in size only to the

Aral Sea on the Kazakhstan-Uzbekistan border. It also is the second-largest *alpine* lake in the world; only Lake Titicaca, in South America, is greater.

Situated in northeastern Kyrgyzstan, Issyk-Kul is a shimmering salt lake about 100 miles (160 kilometers) long, 40 miles (64 km) wide, and more than 2,000 feet (610 meters) deep. It sprawls along a section of the Tian Shan Mountains, from which melting snow drains into the lake. Remarkably, Issyk-Kul does not freeze in winter, a result of its high salt content and the strong winds that constantly trouble its surface. The Kyrgyz people call it the "hot lake." To some of the region's ancient inhabitants, the turquoise lake was a sacred body of water and swimming in it was forbidden. Today the lake faces an environmental threat: traces of poisonous elements from a nearby uranium mine have been detected filtering into it, more than 30 years after the mine ceased operation.

The huge, remote lake served two interesting uses during Kyrgyzstan's period as a Soviet republic. The Soviet navy found it to be a suitable location for testing secret torpedo technology. Meanwhile, health spas brought Soviet vacationers to the lake to enjoy its hot springs and mud baths. Today, the naval project is history, but some of the spas remain. In all, about 120 resorts operate around the lake. The lake is also known as the place where Nikolay Przhevalsky, a famous 19th-century Russian explorer of inner Asia, asked to be buried. This combination of history and natural beauty makes Issyk-Kul the most important tourist attraction of Kyrgyzstan.

In the basin of the Naryn River, which runs westward through the Fergana Valley, there are two fairly large lakes: Chatyr-Kol and Song-Kul. Chatyr-Kol is salty like Issyk-Kul, but neither it nor Song-Kul approaches Issyk-Kul in size.

The country's two major rivers are the Chu, which forms part of the border with Kazakhstan in the north, and the Naryn, which flows through

**A Kyrgyz man looks out onto the Naryn River, which runs through the Fergana Valley in western Kyrgyzstan.**

the Fergana Valley in the west. Because they wind down from steep heights, most of Kyrgyzstan's rivers run swiftly. This feature prohibits the waterways from being navigable, but also makes them ideal for generating hydroelectric power. The Naryn in particular has been heavily developed with hydro projects.

## Central Asia's Prize Valley

The most lush and vibrant area of Kyrgyzstan is the Fergana Valley. More than 180 miles (290 kilometers) long, the valley also spreads over parts of Tajikistan and Uzbekistan. The Fergana contains highly prized fertile land in a region of the world where most of the terrain is harsh by comparison. Today, one of the Kyrgyzstan government's most worrisome dilemmas is the longstanding tension between Kyrgyz and Uzbek peoples over the wealth offered by the Fergana.

Because the valley is so agriculturally important, it has attracted the attention of foreign powers throughout history. During the second cen-

### The Geography of Kyrgyzstan

**Location:** Central Asia on China's western border
**Area:** slightly smaller than South Dakota
   **total:** 76,600 square miles (198,500 sq km)
   **land:** 74,600 square miles (191,300 sq km)
   **water:** 2,808 square miles (7,200 sq km)
**Borders:** China, 532 miles (858 km); Kazakhstan, 652 miles (1,051 km); Tajikistan, 539 miles (870 km); Uzbekistan, 681 miles (1,099 km)
**Climate:** dry continental to polar in the upper Tian Shan Mountains; subtropical in the Fergana Valley; temperate in the northern foothills
**Terrain:** almost completely mountainous
**Elevation extremes:**
   **lowest point:** Kara-Daryya, 433 feet (132 meters)
   **highest point:** Pik Pobedy (Mount Victory), 24,400 feet (7,439 meters)

Source: Adapted from CIA World Factbook, 2004.

tury B.C., the Chinese emperor Wu Ti heard of a horse breed of heavenly descent that thrived in the Fergana Valley. Wu Ti sent a delegation to the area to ask the ruler of Scythia (a region east of the Aral Sea) to give him some of the fabled horses. When the emperor's request was denied, Wu Ti sent an army of 60,000 men to invade the Fergana Valley and take the animals by force. This was a formidable endeavor, as the expedition had to travel 4,000 miles (6,400 km) over a route that included some of the world's most rugged terrain. Thousands of Chinese soldiers died of cold, starvation, and thirst in the merciless Tian Shan Mountains. In the end, the emperor got his horses, though at a colossal human cost.

Later, one of the trading routes between China and Europe passed through the valley, which was occupied by nomadic herders. Descriptions of the Fergana Valley spread with the caravan merchants who traveled the trade routes, which became known collectively as the Silk Road.

Today, as in past eras, Kyrgyzstanis take advantage of the valley's fruitfulness. Through farming they produce items as diverse as cotton, spices, and silk worms and then sell them at bustling markets. But in modern times the Fergana has acquired a dark reputation as the source of another agricultural commodity, opium, which is used in the manufacture of several illegal drugs, including heroin.

Other important valleys, the Chu and Talas, are located in the north of the country. It is in these flat valley districts that most of Kyrgyzstan's limited agriculture is conducted. Altogether, less than 10 percent of Kyrgyzstan's land is suitable for farming, and most of the fertile areas require ***irrigation*** to ensure reliable productivity.

The Chu Valley will potentially play an important role in Kyrgyzstan's economic future for another reason. Scientists think the valley may contain important oil reserves. At present, the Fergana Valley is the country's only oil site, and production is limited.

## A Varied Climate

The country's dominant mountains loom in contrast to the surrounding plains and deserts of neighboring Kazakhstan, Tajikistan, and Uzbekistan. Because of the radical differences in elevation, Kyrgyzstan has a marked range of temperatures. The alpine heights impel inhabitants to bundle in warm clothing much of the year—especially in winter, when frigid winds blow down from the north and the country's average temperature is –5° Fahrenheit (–20° Celsius). In the higher mountains, the average winter temperature is even colder at –18°F (–28°C). Some of Kyrgyzstan's deep valleys, flanked by steep mountain slopes, receive only a few hours of daily sunshine. The coldest temperatures are recorded in these parts of the country.

At the opposite extreme, certain lowland parts of Kyrgyzstan are seasonal hot spots where summer temperatures reach 90°F (32°C). Generally, July temperatures average 60°F to 75°F (16°C to 24°C) in the valleys and **steppes**, while the mountains warm up to about 40°F (4°C).

Overall, Kyrgyzstan receives adequate rain and snowfall to support life. Annual precipitation ranges from about 4 to 40 inches (10 to 102 centimeters), depending on the region.

## Problems Posed by Terrain and Other Natural Conditions

Kyrgyzstan is a country of natural grandeur, but it has encountered problems related to its geographical features. In recent years, these problems have brought attention to the need for better management of its natural resources.

Although Kyrgyzstan's human population is sparse compared to many other nations, the society nonetheless has had a negative impact on the land and water. Overgrazing by large herds of livestock has eroded the soil

**Some of Kyrgyzstan's environmental problems date back to the Soviet era. The signs in this photograph warn about the danger of radioactivity at this site near the Maili Suu River, which is at the head of the Fergana Valley in southwestern Kyrgyzstan. The radioactive contamination came from a Soviet uranium processing plant; the grass-covered mounds in the background contain uranium waste dumped between 1948 and 1968.**

in many areas. During the last few decades, the country experienced a trend toward having more livestock than the pastureland could support. The effect of lost topsoil and grass cover will likely worsen in the future. Another problem has been caused by hydroelectric development. Much prime farmland was sacrificed, for example, when the Naryn River was flooded to create the Toktogol Reservoir.

These kinds of problems are especially hard for the government to solve. Hydroelectric power is necessary, not just to supply Kyrgyzstan's

> **Kyrgyzstan's Tian Shan Mountains are both spectacular and dangerous. In modern times, mountain climbers have lost their lives attempting to scale some of the alluring peaks.**

people but also to generate income through its sale to other countries. And as in past centuries, many Kyrgyz today depend on livestock herds for their livelihoods. To restrict those activities would worsen the country's already troubled economy.

Conversely, Kyrgyzstan's geographical features—its mountains, in particular—have a negative effect on the people by creating physical barriers that keep groups separated. Kyrgyzstan thus has two primary population centers: the Chu River valley (which includes Bishkek) in the north and the Fergana region (which includes Osh) in the southwest. The inhabitants of these areas, for the most part, live separate lives, with different ethnic backgrounds and different approaches to Islam. They have differing and complex ties with neighboring countries and with Russia, which today remains a key international partner. They earn their livings in different ways, and they have contradictory expectations of their government.

Over the years, the two regions have evolved almost as individual republics. Transportation, for example, has progressed as two connected but basically separate systems. South of the mountains, Osh is linked by rails and highways to neighboring cities and to the transportation systems of Uzbekistan. The northern cities, meanwhile, are similarly linked with one another, and their transportation routes are tied into those of Kazakhstan. In addition to this one major division, the rough mountain terrain of Kyrgyzstan's mountains keeps villages isolated and remote, with limited transportation access.

With its natural wonders and physical obstacles, the geography of Kyrgyzstan is both an asset and a burden. If the new Kyrgyz Republic is to establish itself as a stable nation, it must find ways to take advantage of its geography while overcoming the difficulties posed by the landscape and resolving its environmental concerns.

A stele, or engraved stone pillar, carved by Kyrgyz warriors. These monuments can be found throughout some parts of Kyrgyzstan. The Kyrgyz migrated to this area of Central Asia more than a thousand years ago, although scientists have found evidence that humans lived in the region as far back as the Stone Age.

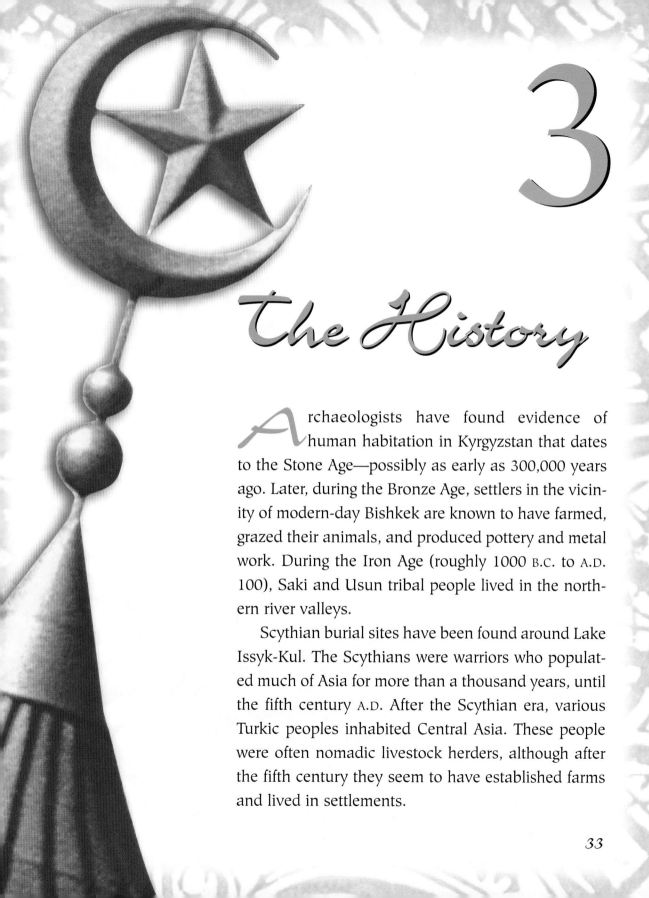

# 3

# The History

rchaeologists have found evidence of human habitation in Kyrgyzstan that dates to the Stone Age—possibly as early as 300,000 years ago. Later, during the Bronze Age, settlers in the vicinity of modern-day Bishkek are known to have farmed, grazed their animals, and produced pottery and metal work. During the Iron Age (roughly 1000 B.C. to A.D. 100), Saki and Usun tribal people lived in the northern river valleys.

Scythian burial sites have been found around Lake Issyk-Kul. The Scythians were warriors who populated much of Asia for more than a thousand years, until the fifth century A.D. After the Scythian era, various Turkic peoples inhabited Central Asia. These people were often nomadic livestock herders, although after the fifth century they seem to have established farms and lived in settlements.

# On the Trade Routes

The land that is now Kyrgyzstan encompassed the northern section of the Silk Road trade route. Beginning around the first century B.C., merchants from Persia and the Mediterranean region established a thriving trade for silk cloth from China. Silk, a fabric that was highly valued both in China and the West, is woven from the fibers of silkworm cocoons. The Chinese nourished the worms on mulberry leaves anda produced these fabrics by a secret process.

"Just as oil is the liquid gold of the present, so silk was the most important article not only of trade but also of payment in China," observes historian Richard N. Frye in his book *The Heritage of Central Asia*. "Nomads were persuaded to stop their raids by presents of rolls or bolts of silk from

**This detail from a map drawn in 1375 shows a caravan traveling the Silk Road. This name—which was not coined until the 19th century—is used to refer to a network of trade routes that linked China with Persia and the civilizations of the Mediterranean Sea.**

Many of Kyrgyzstan's towns and cities, including the capital, Bishkek, originated as forts and outposts. From ancient times, a military presence has been required not only to ensure control over the people by the ruling power, but to protect traders. Merchants who passed through the region were targets of brigands who lay in wait at secluded places along the remote trade routes.

the Chinese court. Likewise special services by individuals to the Chinese state were rewarded with gifts of silk."

The trade routes extending through Central Asia and the Middle East were dangerous and rough, especially in Central Asia. Aside from the difficult terrain, robbers lay in wait for caravans. However, to adventurous merchants the great wealth that trading offered was well worth the risk.

The silk trade flourished during the Roman era. Prosperous Roman citizens could afford to buy the prized cloth, and they demanded more and more of it. The Sogdians, who lived mainly in what is now northern Tajikistan, were among the leading silk merchants.

It was more than the long-distance silk trade with China that brought Central Asians into contact with foreigners. By the 10th century, Kyrgyz nomads began migrating from a region in present-day Russia into parts of what are now Kyrgyzstan and Kazakhstan. The Kyrgyz are believed to have conducted trade with other groups in various regions of Central Asia including southern Siberia and Tibet.

During the 12th century A.D., the Tian Shan Mountains were the domain of the Kara Khitai. These people had been driven from northern China and established a short-lived empire that reached westward into Muslim lands. Like so many other inhabitants of Central Asia, they eventually succumbed to the powerful Mongols.

## The Mongol Hordes

During the early 13th century Central Asia became part of the empire of the Mongol warlord Genghis Khan, one of the greatest conquerors the world has ever known. By the time of his death, Genghis Khan ruled a domain that stretched from the coast of China to the Caspian Sea at the southeastern fringe of Europe.

The great leader was born around 1167. He was originally named Temujin, and was the son of a Mongol tribal chief. When Temujin was about 13, his father was killed. Athough Temujin was in line to become the new chief, he and his family were overlooked because others in the tribe did not want to have a young boy as leader. They were forced to leave the tribe, and for several years the family struggled to survive.

As he grew to manhood, Temujin attracted a band of followers. He developed an army by forging alliances and conquering other groups. Temujin proved to be a shrewd diplomat as well as a stern commander, and by the early 1200s the Mongols declared him Genghis Khan, the "universal ruler."

Genghis then turned his attention abroad, conquering northern China, Central Asia, and territories to the west controlled by Arab Muslims. His hordes of cavalry seemed practically invincible. If a city or kingdom in their path refused to surrender peacefully, it was annihilated. The Mongol invaders slew whole populations. Among peoples who submitted to the conquerors,

**During the 13th century, Genghis Khan led the Mongols in their conquest of most of Central Asia. By the time of his death in 1227, the Mongols ruled a larger land area than any other empire in history.**

the Mongols established chieftains to rule over territorial divisions called **khanates**. Most people regard the Mongol hordes as among the most ruthless of the world's conquerors.

Genghis Khan's army became less and less Mongol in identity and more **cosmopolitan** as the empire grew. Many Turkic tribes joined the Khan's armies, and the defeated—who included Kyrgyz men—were added to the original force. The Kyrgyz, who were then living in the Yenisey River area, submitted to the Mongols between 1207 and 1209.

## The Kyrgyz People

The Kyrgyz people did not originate in the territory that now bears their name. They migrated from an undetermined place to the north. According to ancient Chinese records, ancestors of the Kyrgyz may have lived in northwestern Mongolia as early as 4,000 years ago, possibly among the outside marauders who harassed Chinese settlements. These invaders eventually prompted the Chinese to begin erecting the Great Wall around 221 B.C.

Over time these people were scattered. The word *Kirgiz* was used in the eighth century in reference to inhabitants of the upper Yenisey River, north of present-day Mongolia and northeast of modern Kyrgyzstan. Between the 10th and 16th centuries, some of the people moved—or were pushed—southward by powerful armies, including the Mongols. They came to be dominated by the Golden Horde, the group of Mongols who established control over Russia and parts of Central Asia under the leadership of Genghis Khan's grandson Batu Khan in 1251. (After Genghis Khan's death in 1227, the Mongol Empire was divided into four sections, called *ulus*. Control over each of these was given to one of Genghis Khan's descendants, with a great khan continuing to rule the entire empire.)

The Kyrgyz were nomads who mainly lived a primitive lifestyle, though evidence suggests their culture showed sophisticated advances such as plated armor and extended trade channels into other regions.

Over the centuries the Kyrgyz adopted Islam, a religion that had developed on the Arabian Peninsula in the seventh century A.D. Islam is based on the teachings of the prophet Muhammad. Believers say that around the year 610, Muhammad received messages from God, or Allah, while the prophet was meditating in the mountains near modern-day Mecca, Saudi Arabia. Muhammad explained Allah's teachings to the Arab tribes over the next 22 years, eventually uniting many of them under his leadership. After his death, followers began to spread the religion beyond the Arabian Peninsula. At first, Islam spread throughout the Middle East, northern Africa, and into Persia by conquering armies. After the ninth century, the religion spread deeper into Central Asia primarily through the work of Muslim missionaries and traders.

The wealthy centers of Arab Islamic civilization that emerged with the religion's development also fell to the Mongols as they pressed through Central Asia. In 1258, Mongols under Hulegü Khan sacked Baghdad, at the time the center of the Arab dynasty that ruled many of the Muslim lands. The fall of the Abbasid dynasty marked the end of Arab control of an Islamic empire, and Arab lands were divided among Mongols and the Mamluks of Egypt. But Islam still thrived under Mongol rule, and by 1313 the Mongol rulers of Central Asia converted, making Islam the official religion of their empire.

"The fall of Baghdad had shown the debility of Islam as a state—but it was a state that was far more than a body of political rules and customs," writes historian Desmond Stewart. "Islam was also a society. As a society, it had strengths and weaknesses. The latter brought about its defeat at the hands of pagan conquerors; the former, in a very short time, turned the conquerors into ardent Muslims."

At its height the Mongol Empire covered an area five times larger than the ancient Macedonian empire of Alexander the Great (356–323 B.C.). However, the united Mongol state could not survive for long against pressure from a rising power in the West, the Ottoman Turks, or from the resurgent Chinese Ming dynasty in the East. The Golden Horde maintained power after the rest of the empire collapsed, but by the 15th century united Russian tribes had largely eliminated the Mongols' control.

During the next three centuries the Kyrgyz people were dominated by various groups, including Kalmyks, Manchus, and Uzbeks. In the 1700s, the Kokand khanate of the Uzbeks occupied the southeastern part of Central Asia, which includes what is now Kyrgyzstan. The years of its rule are remembered for the oppression and brutality that the native tribes suffered. Repeated Kyrgyz uprisings all were defeated.

The armies of the Russian tsar helped expand Russia's claim to territory in the broad steppes north of the Aral Sea, in what is now Kazakhstan, during the 1700s. By the middle of the next century, the armies had advanced into the lower regions of Central Asia. Although some Kyrgyz had accepted the oppressive Kokand yoke and even held administrative posts within the khanate, most were willing to negotiate with Russia in order to free themselves of Uzbek oppression. Russian forces defeated the Kokand khanate in 1876. What is now Kyrgyzstan became part of Russia's Central Asian colony, known as Russian Turkistan.

## Life Under the Tsars

At first, many native Kyrgyz welcomed the Russians after suffering the harsh treatment of the Kokand khanate. Through the skills and resources of the Russians, houses, roads, and schools were built and living conditions improved. However, these changes were not made to help the original inhabitants, but to benefit Russian settlers who moved into Russian Turkistan. The Russians were simply establishing their own lifestyle in their new colony. Although they showed some interest in native cultures—the earliest known books printed in the Kyrgyz language date from this period, for example—they were not concerned with providing equal living conditions for Asians and Europeans. Kyrgyz and other tribal peoples continued to live much the way their ancestors had lived. Most remained illiterate.

Soon, Central Asians became unhappy with conditions under the rule of the Russian tsar. Nomadic herders were losing much of their pastureland to Russian and Ukrainian settlers, especially in the northern part of the region. The Asians were unjustly taxed, and Russian merchants, who controlled many essential products, charged unfair prices.

During World War I, the growing resentment of the Central Asians toward Russia increased. Although they were exempt from fighting for the Russian army, many still were required to work as noncombatants to assist Russia's war effort. The Kyrgyz and others felt European affairs had nothing to do with them, and they were being forced to support the interests of the Russian settlers who had taken their ancestral lands. In 1916, the Kyrgyz, Kazakhs, Uzbeks, and other peoples of Central Asia revolted against the tsar's authority. Uprisings occurred at Pishpek (the former name of Bishkek) and other towns. Russian settlers banded together in response, aided by the tsarist army. The fighting was widespread and bloody. "By the time reinforcements put an end to the rebellion, it was estimated that 2,000 settlers perished, but even greater numbers of local people were killed," writes historian Hélène Carrère d'Encausse. "Entire Kirgiz villages had been put to the torch, and nearly a third of the Kirgiz population had fled to China." By one estimate, at least 100,000 Kyrgyz—about an eighth of the ethnic group's estimated population—died in the affair.

## The Soviet Era

The 1916 Central Asian uprising was one of several revolts against the tsarist dynasty. In 1905, Russian workers had threatened a revolution, which forced the tsar to make some accomodations to their wishes. When World War I began in August 1914, Russia entered the fighting on the side

**This photograph shows a Kyrgyz woman and her children outside of the family's yurt, circa 1900. As the Russian tsars brought Central Asia into their vast empire during the late 19th century, most of the Kyrgyz attempted to retain their traditional way of life.**

of England and France against its historic enemy, Germany. Initially the Russian people supported the war, but as battlefield casualties mounted in horrifying numbers, and people at home faced starvation and appalling conditions, public opinion turned against the Russian rulers. In the minds of most Russians, Tsar Nicholas II was to blame for their misfortunes.

Nicholas abdicated after an uprising in St. Petersburg, the Russian capital, early in 1917. By the end of the year, the Bolsheviks, led by Vladimir Ilyich Lenin, had taken control of the country. The Bolsheviks were communist followers of the teachings of Karl Marx, and their leaders promised the weary masses "bread, peace, and land" as they imposed a Communist government. Over the next few years the Communists fought

**Vladimir Lenin (1870–1924), left, and Joseph Stalin (1879–1953) were two founding leaders of the Bolshevik party. This photograph was taken in 1922, the year the Union of Soviet Socialist Republics (U.S.S.R.) was formed. After Lenin's death, Stalin emerged from a struggle for power as the U.S.S.R.'s sole ruler in 1929. Stalin's policies—particularly collectivization and repression of Kyrgyz culture and the practice of Islam—had a terrible effect on traditional life in the region.**

with other groups for control over Russia. By 1922 the Bolshevik revolution was complete, and the tsarist empire was reconstituted as the Union of Soviet Socialist Republics (U.S.S.R.). The new leadership mandated that all property, businesses, and industries belonged to the state and were subject to Communist Party authority.

In the early 1920s, the Soviet leadership forged several alignments of Kirghizia and other Central Asian regions that had been part of the tsarist empire. Kirghizia was made an autonomous ***oblast***, or subdivision of a republic, in 1925, and an autonomous republic the following year. It attained the status of a full republic in 1936, and would remain part of the U.S.S.R. until 1991.

The years following the Bolshevik creation of the Soviet Union were uncertain, brutal, and tragic throughout the Central Asian republics. Government officials and citizens who opposed the Bolsheviks were executed or sent to remote labor camps. Many dissidents simply disappeared, their fates unknown. These victims even included people who had supported the revolution but later found themselves, through changes in power and policies, on the wrong side of the prevailing leadership. Meanwhile, ethnic Kyrgyz continued to flee the country into China.

The ruling party in Moscow dealt harshly with local leaders who criticized the new union of republics. In the Kirghiz Autonomous Oblast in 1925, a group of Communist leaders called the Thirty lodged a protest against the Russification of Kirghizia. They were unhappy that Russian Communists had been given important positions and that official transactions had to be conducted in Russian. They also complained that ethnic Kyrgyz were being neglected or mistreated. In response to the complaints, the government removed the Thirty from the Communist Party and banished their leader from Khirgizia. Other dissidents were imprisoned not long afterward.

## Forced Allegiance to the Soviet State

Although the Soviet Union's 15 republics were comprised of people with widely varied languages, customs, and traditions, the regime in Moscow tried to force a spirit of union among all the ethnic groups. It attempted to replace ancient loyalties to culture and religion with a single allegiance—to the state. People living in the republics were not permitted to rely on their local leadership or glorify their national histories. They were instructed to learn the Russian language. Writers and poets were criticized and censored—and sometimes even arrested—if their work seemed in any way anti-Russian or threatening to Communist Party doctrine. All traditions of folk culture were stifled (for the Kyrgyz, this primarily meant repression of the long-recited stories of the hero Manas).

Many people in the Soviet republics continued to resist Russification, particularly those in Central Asia. This region was opposed largely because more than three-fourths of the people living there were Muslims, who are wary of any government that is atheistic (does not believe in the existence of God). Most Central Asians continued to communicate in their own ethnic languages, not in Russian. As a result, in spite of their Soviet citizenship they lived in a world apart from Soviet society. Their histories and cultures were similar to one another, yet very different from the histories and cultures of the republics throughout the Soviet Union.

Although the political resistance in Khirgizia, represented by the Thirty, had little success during the 1920s, the general populace won certain exceptions from Russification. The Kyrgyz were allowed to continue traditional cultural practices and, to an extent, live under the administration of Kyrgyz leaders.

The situation changed, however, after Joseph Stalin vanquished his political rivals and seized full control of the U.S.S.R. in 1929. Stalin ruled the Soviet Union with a heavy hand, insisting that all the people in every republic follow his political principles. His infamous legacy in Central Asia was a policy of **collectivization**—forcing nomadic tribes onto state-owned farms. During the 1930s, some of Kirghizia's governmental and Communist Party leaders were executed, and the purging of party officials occurred periodically in the 1940s and 1950s.

Still, a large segment of Kirghizia's younger generation appreciated Russification. They believed, as the authorities taught them, that the Russian way of life represented progress. It was true that improvements were made in health care, education, and industrialization, and that over the decades, Kyrgyzstanis began to enjoy a higher standard of living than they had under the tsars. Nonetheless, overall the Central Asian republics remained the least urbanized in the U.S.S.R. In time, most people of the region became disenchanted with the Soviet system.

During the 1980s, the republics' general support for the Communist system declined, as a program of reforms instituted by Mikhail Gorbachev weakened the power of the Communist Party and the Soviet government. Native peoples of the Central Asian republics became increasingly bold in protesting Russian supremacy. They were especially angry over the Soviet practice of giving the best jobs and most important titles to ethnic Russians. At a 1988 meeting of Kyrgyz writers, speakers voiced frustration at Moscow's intolerant policies toward Kyrgyz beliefs and customs, and toward Islam.

## Independence

As part of a growing movement toward self-government, the Supreme Soviet, the assembly of Communist leaders that ruled the republic, changed the name of the republic in 1990 from Kirghizia to Kyrgyzstan. Some members of the ruling body by that time were also demanding that Kyrgyz become the republic's official language.

That same year, the Supreme Soviet selected Askar Akayev to be the republic's president. Akayev, a liberal on the reform wing of the ailing Communist Party, was a follower of Gorbachev's reform movement. He did not initially advocate independence; instead, he shared with Gorbachev a belief that the Soviet Union could be saved if it underwent the right reforms. When a coup was attempted against Gorbachev in August 1991, Akayev immediately denounced the conspirators.

The push toward independence was too strong to ignore, however. Violence between ethnic Uzbeks and Kyrgyz outside Osh in 1990 signaled instability. The spirit of resistance that was evident in Kazakhstan and other Central Asian republics motivated Kyrgyz leaders, and Kyrgyzstan followed several other states by declaring its independence on August 31, 1991. Akayev, running unopposed, was elected president by popular vote in October. Kyrgyzstan officially became an independent republic when the Soviet Union disbanded in December of that year. The new republic adopted its constitution in May 1993.

Although the Soviet Union was no more, something akin to it soon appeared in the form of the Commonwealth of Independent States (CIS). This is a loose alliance of most of the former Soviet republics, including Kyrgyzstan. The exact nature and purpose of the CIS has not been completely agreed upon, as political leaders in the former republics have expressed different ideas about what the CIS should or should not do. While it exercises no controlling power, the CIS has had significant influence as the new governments strive for their countries' stability.

## Into the 21st Century

Although the collapse of the Soviet Union led to independence for the Central Asian republics, overall it has brought the people no great benefits. In some ways, conditions have become bleaker than they were under Soviet rule.

Of the five Central Asian republics, Kyrgyzstan has been the most progressive in many ways. National and regional leaders have made vigorous efforts to obtain foreign assistance and establish beneficial relations with many countries, and in 1998 Kyrgyzstan became the first of the five to join the World Trade Organization, an international group that seeks to reduce trade barriers between countries.

Despite these efforts to enter the global marketplace, Kyrgyzstan's economy has not been strong enough to compete. Production and other economic trends dropped off sharply during the first years of independence. Although the situation stabilized somewhat in the late 1990s, by 1999 Kyrgyzstan's foreign debt had topped $1 billion. By 2006 the country's economy remained troubled by high unemployment and low production.

The nation's political situation is similarly troublesome. Akayev was often accused of running the country in a heavy-handed way. For

**Leaders and ministers of countries from the Commonwealth of Independent States (CIS) gather for a meeting during a 2003 summit in Yalta, Ukraine. After the collapse of the Soviet Union in 1991, the CIS was formed; today the organization's members work together on trade and security issues.**

example, in 1996 he secured controversial changes to Kyrgyzstan's constitution through a referendum. One of the foremost changes was that Akayev won sole authority to appoint most government officials, thus strengthening the power of the president at the expense of other branches of government. Political stress was heightened by the activity of Islamic militants, who operate primarily in the southern provinces, or oblasts. In early 2000, Kyrgyz law enforcement agencies began arresting militant individuals considered to be security threats.

Another volatile issue was the government's aggressive response to protest or opposition. In March 2002, police killed several demonstra-

**The killing of demonstrators in Aksy in March 2002 touched off protests throughout the country, such as this June 2002 rally in Jalal-Abad, a town in southern Kyrgyzstan.**

tors in the southern district of Aksy during a march protesting the imprisonment of opposition leader Azimbek Beknazarov. The event sparked a nationwide uproar; many feared Kyrgyzstan was on the brink of civil war. Tensions eventually eased, but some elected officials continued to demand that the police be punished for their actions in Aksy.

Elections for a new legislature were held in February and March of 2005. Many residents considered these elections rigged, and widespread protests erupted. On March 24, Akayev fled the country; he officially resigned his position on April 4, 2005. The bloodless coup became known as the Tulip Revolution. An interim government was formed, headed by Kurmanbek Bakiyev, a former prime minister who had been forced to resign his position after the 2002 police shootings in Aksy and had become an opponent of the Akayev government.

On July 10, Bakiyev easily won an election as the new president of Kyrgyzstan, receiving more than 88 percent of the vote. However, popular support for the new government had declined by early 2006, as the Bakiyev administration seemed just as unable to deal with corruption and economic problems as the Akayev regime had been.

Askar Akayev, president of Kyrgyzstan, casts his ballot during the October 2000 presidential election. Akayev won with more than 74 percent of the vote; however, international observers complained that elections in Kyrgyzstan were not "free and fair." Concern over rigged elections led to the Tulip Revolution in 2005, when the Akayev government was overthrown.

# 4

# The Economy, Politics, and Religion

*K*yrgyzstan was the second-poorest of the former Central Asian republics when the Soviet Union dissolved. (Only Tajikistan was in worse condition.) Since 1991, Kyrgyzstan's greatest difficulty has been to develop a stable economy for its people.

## Living Off the Land

Although only about 7 percent of the land in Kyrgyzstan is **arable**, the country's economy is mostly agricultural. Livestock herders, like their distant ancestors, still use the upland slopes in the Talas oblast and elsewhere to graze their animals. Herds of sheep provide wool and meat for the owners, as well as commodities to be sold in Kyrgyz cities and international markets. Large herds of goats also are seen on the slopes. The natives breed horses both for transportation and draft work, and as a meat source. Yaks are valuable for carrying heavy loads and for providing meat as well as milk; their long hair is useful in making mats and cloth.

Crops, both for subsistence and for sale, have been important throughout the area's history. In fertile valleys at lower elevations, farmers grow tobacco and cotton—the country's two most important export crops. Vegetable farming also is common, and hayfields provide food for livestock. At harvest time, fresh foods abound at marketplaces in Kyrgyzstan's towns and cities.

For the most part, large-scale farming in Kyrgyzstan has only been possible through irrigation. Bountiful rivers and lakes have given the country an advantage over other Central Asian countries in building irrigation systems. During the first part of the 20th century, irrigation projects in Central Asia were started but then development was stalled for lack of funds. As a result, grain crops dwindled, and in turn the Kyrgyz nomads' sheep, goat, and cattle herds were reduced dramatically.

Another cause of the decline in livestock numbers was the collectivization of land. During Stalin's years in power, the Soviets mandated the socialization of private lands, the settlement of nomadic herders, and the clearing and irrigation of pastureland for crops. Families and whole villages were placed in collective farms and forced to work together. Many of them resisted this policy and were brutally persecuted. Masses of peasants—as many as 15 million, by some accounts—died throughout the Soviet Union during the collectivization of the late 1920s and early 1930s.

Livestock numbers recovered during the middle of the century. Today, it is estimated that Kyrgyzstan has approximately twice as many sheep and goats—about 10 million—as people. There are some 2 million horses and yaks and smaller numbers of swine. As more and more Kyrgyz have

**Shepherds move their flock across the high meadows of western Kyrgyzstan. Herding is a main source of income for Kyrgyzstanis; today, it is estimated that the country has about twice as much livestock as people.**

returned to herding for income, herds have grown and overgrazing has become a problem.

The Moscow regime encouraged certain types of agricultural development throughout Central Asia, especially cotton growing. It did not build processing plants there, however. Fertile areas of the region's republics were used simply to grow the raw products, which were shipped to other republics for processing. This arrangement had serious consequences after independence, as the former republics did not have the factories or infrastructure to establish a strong industrial economy.

In addition, serious ecological problems have resulted from past agricultural practices. For example, the heavy fertilization of chemicals year after year has left much of the land and water polluted. In turn, this has endangered the citizens' health.

## The Economy of Kyrgyzstan

**Gross domestic product (GDP\*):** $9.324 billion

**GDP per capita:** $1,800

**Inflation:** 4.2%

**Natural resources:** hydroelectric power; gold and other rare metals; raw energy sources including coal, oil, and natural gas; mineral deposits including mercury, nepheline, bismuth, zinc, and lead

**Agriculture (37% of GDP):** tobacco, cotton, potatoes, vegetables, grapes, fruits and berries, wool, sheep, goats, cattle.

**Industry (22% of GDP):** small machinery, textiles, food processing, cement, shoes, sawn logs, refrigerators, furniture, electric motors, gold, rare earth metals.

**Services (41% of GDP):** government, banking, tourism, other.

**Foreign trade:**

   **Imports**—$937.4 million: oil and gas, machinery and equipment, chemicals, foodstuffs

   **Exports**—$759 million: cotton, wool, meat, tobacco, gold, mercury, uranium, natural gas, hydropower, machinery, shoes

**Currency exchange rate (2005):** U.S. $1 = 40.13 Kyrgyzstan soms

\*GDP, or gross domestic product, is the total value of goods and services produced in a country annually.

All figures are 2005 estimates unless otherwise noted.

Sources: Bloomberg.com; CIA World Factbook, 2005.

Still, agricultural production was comparatively high in most Central Asian countries at the time of independence. The economies of some regional republics have been supplemented by crude oil and gas, though not Kyrgyzstan's. Instead, it has done the best it can with a limited, farm-based economy.

## Other Economic Assets

The production of different minerals have played a role in the region's economy for centuries. Iron mines were operated in this part of Central Asia before the Mongol era. Coal mining became important during the 20th century; Soviet Kirghizia produced more than 3 million metric tons of coal in 1963. However, coal production, which was supported by the Soviet government before independence, dropped dramatically during the 1990s, as did production in other areas. The country still has sizeable coal deposits, which Kyrgyz officials believe can be tapped if foreign investors can be found. Other important mineral exports today include gold, mercury, and uranium.

Light industries were developed during the Soviet period. Kyrgyz companies produce machinery, electrical items, and processed foods. Wool, cotton, leather goods, and silk garments are produced in quantities significant enough to be exported.

Hydroelectric projects were developed on the Naryn River in the mid-1900s. The country gets its own electric power from hydro plants and is able to sell and trade some of the power it generates. With Kazakhstan, the neighbor to the north, Kyrgyzstan has exchanged this energy for much-needed coal.

Lake Issyk-Kul supports a small fishing industry. It is known for its large trout, some of which grow to weigh more than 70 pounds (32 kilograms).

## Independence and New Challenges

Kyrgyzstan entered its era of independence with a mixture of hope and despair. It was free after years of overbearing Soviet control, but it was by no means a prosperous country. Industrial production dropped by more than half in the first three years of independence, the result of two damaging factors: the emigration of many Russian skilled laborers back to their homeland and a dearth of energy to run the manufacturing plants. A gasoline shortage in the mid-1990s restricted highway travel.

Unemployment and low incomes were basic problems at independence, and these problems remain. Ordinary items sometimes are hard to obtain. In his account of travels through Central Asia, *The Lost Heart of Asia*, travel writer Colin Thubron recounts a conversation he had with a Kyrgyz writer in Bishkek: "We've hundreds of writers, but no money . . . and our publishers can't get paper," lamented the native. "It used to come to us from Russia, but now everything's atrophied. So at last we have our freedom to write— but no paper! . . . There was always too much that we couldn't say. We couldn't draw on our traditions or write our own history. Now our spiritual situation is richer, far richer, but our material one is hopeless."

In late 1991, Kyrgyzstan established an independent banking system. The country introduced its own currency, the som, in 1993. One result was the reduction of the nation's alarming inflation rate, which had risen as high as 88 percent. The economy began to strengthen in the mid-1990s, with increased production and exports. As it entered the 21st century, Kyrgyzstan had managed to lower and stabilize inflation. Between 2001 and 2003, its inflation rate ranged from about 2 to 7 percent, though wages can barely keep pace with these rates.

The introduction of the som also had negative effects, however. In particular, it angered the governments of neighboring Uzbekistan and Kazakhstan. They feared the new currency would further upset the stability of the Russian ruble, which already was in trouble, and thus would increase inflation throughout the region. Uzbekistan, at the time one of Kyrgyzstan's principal trading partners, responded by temporarily cutting off its supply of gas and other vital products to Kyrgyzstan.

## Extraordinary Measures

In the face of these obstacles, President Akayev took extraordinary steps to improve the economy. Breaking away from the previous system of government ownership of property, he allowed apartment dwellings and some state farms to become privately owned. He sought expertise in economic matters from the International Monetary Fund (IMF) and from western leaders, and encouraged foreigners to invest in Kyrgyzstan's industry. A 1997 agreement with Germany, for instance, offered German investors tax benefits in Kyrgyzstan. Other joint ventures were arranged with businesses in China, the United States, Turkey, Britain, and other countries.

The parliament adopted a law allowing certain state-run businesses and industries to be sold to private owners. A fund was created to help private citizens obtain loans to buy such enterprises without having to pay interest.

**The Toktogul hydroelectric dam on the Naryn River was built by the Soviet Union in 1975. Facilities such as this one produce more electricity than Kyrgyzstan can use, thus enabling the country to sell the surplus to its neighbors.**

Such measures achieved a degree of success. Between 1991 and 1993, the ownership structures of more than 4,000 Kyrgyzstani businesses and other entities were altered. A few foreign business enterprises decided to become involved in Kyrgyzstan projects. For example, a Canadian company took on the development of a Kyrgyzstan gold field. However, these economic reforms saw results that were, for the most part, disappointing. Among the newly privatized businesses, almost half were found to be operating at a loss in 1996. Mismanagement and government corruption in the early years hampered economic development.

Another hindrance to Kyrgyzstan's economy is the country's remote location, which makes it difficult to conduct international commerce and only attracts a modest level of investment. An economic crisis in Russia in 1998 had a devastating effect on Kyrgyzstan and other Central Asian countries. Finally, a growing population has put increasing stress on the number of available jobs. The population boom was aggravated during the mid-1990s, when refugees from a war in neighboring Tajikistan fled into Kyrgyzstan.

## Tourism: A Glimmer of Hope

Tourism has been slow to develop in Kyrgyzstan, but it could help the country's economy improve. The country is becoming recognized as a tourist destination, for mountain climbers and backpackers in particular. It also lures skiers, some of whom come for the unique experience of skiing the Ak-Say glaciers of Ala-Archa nature park, located north of Bishkek.

Already, some rural Kyrgyz families are earning cash by journeying to Bishkek at the height of the tourist season. They set up their yurts outside the city and sell handmade souvenirs such as *kalpaks* (native hats) to foreigners. In certain rural locales, mountain inhabitants rent their horses to tourists for exploring the canyons and hills.

However, many would-be tourists are leery because Kyrgyzstan's tourist industry is woefully undeveloped. Only in certain areas of the mountains and in the north, around Bishkek and Lake Issyk-Kul, are services and facilities consistent. Elsewhere, visitors find that the limited modes of transportation can make travel expensive and, with crime on the rise, dangerous. Many roads are not patrolled by the authorities. According to recent reports, it is especially risky for foreigners in the southwestern part of the country, where tensions run high between Kyrgyz and Uzbeks.

## A New Government

Kyrgyzstan has a representative form of government, with branches of authority similar to those in many western government structures. The president holds more power than any other leader in the country.

The country's constitution, ratified in 1993, promised equality and granted considerable freedom to citizens. It established an elected parliament, which through amendment was later split into two separate bodies. The Assembly of People's Representatives has 70 seats, with members elected from specific regions. The Legislative Assembly has 35 seats, with members elected nationwide. Representatives to both bodies are chosen in popular elections to serve five-year terms.

Kyrgyzstan is divided into six administrative provinces, called oblasts. The president appoints the governor of each oblast. There also is a city administrative district, known as a *shaar*, in Bishkek.

The country's legal system is a hierarchical structure. Above its local and regional courts are a Supreme Court, a Constitutional Court, and a Higher Court of Arbitration. A Supreme Economic Court decides higher cases involving commercial issues. The president nominates Supreme Court judges, but they must be approved and appointed by the legislative bodies.

Kyrgyzstan, like some of its Central Asian neighbors, maintains a small military. This consists of army, air defense, security, and border patrol personnel. Initially, the government planned to not have a standing army but

**The flag of Kyrgyzstan consists of a red field with a yellow sun; the 40 rays emanating from the sun represent the 40 traditional Kyrgyz tribes. The stylized image in the center of the sun represents the roof of a yurt. The flag was adopted in March 1992, shortly after Kyrgyzstan declared independence.**

nationwide. Representatives to both bodies were chosen in popular elections to serve five-year terms. In 2005, new elections were held for a 75-seat unicamerial parliament that would replace the bicameral assembly. These elections were widely viewed as corrupt, and led to the Tulip Revolution that overthew the Akayev government.

In 2005, Bakiyev announced that a referendum would be held to determine how power would be distributed between the president and the assembly. That referendum was tentatively scheduled for 2006.

The country's legal system is a hierarchical structure. Above its local and regional courts are a Supreme Court, a Constitutional Court, and a Higher Court of Arbitration. A Supreme Economic Court decides higher cases involving commercial issues. The president nominates Supreme Court judges, but they must be approved and appointed by the legislative bodies.

Kyrgyzstan is divided into seven administrative provinces, called oblasts. The president appoints the governor of each oblast. There also is a city administrative district, known as a *shaar*, in Bishkek.

Kyrgyzstan, like some of its Central Asian neighbors, maintains a small military. This consists of army, air defense, security, and border patrol personnel. Initially, the government planned to not have a standing army but to instead rely on the security of the Commonwealth of Independent States. In 1992, Kyrgyzstan decided to establish an army of about 8,000. By 1996, it had some 12,000 ground troops, 4,000 air defense personnel, 2,000 border security officers, a centralized police force of 25,000, and a government security guard of 1,000. Kyrgyzstan has had to bolster its border forces, largely because of factional clashes in the southwest. Still, in 2001 its military spending was a modest amount—approximately $20 million. This total was less than the budgets of many American corporations.

## Government History in Kyrgyzstan

Because Communism was considered the only legitimate political affiliation in the Soviet Union, the Communist Party of Kirgiziya (CPK) basically ran the government of the republic during the Soviet era. With the demise of the U.S.S.R. and the advent of popular elections, the CPK became the People's Democratic Party and lost power as Kyrgyzstan developed its multiparty political system.

At the time Kyrgyzstan became independent, some observers considered its government to be the most open and politically tolerant in Central Asia. The government took steps to transform a policy of government-held property to private ownership. Even before Kirgizia broke away from the Soviet Union, most of its legislative seats were won in closely contested elections—a strong indication of democratic governance. As president of the new republic, Akayev permitted the publication of independent news-

**The arrest of opposition leader Feliks Kulov was an example of how the Akayev government used its power to repress dissent. In this 2002 photo, activists outside the presidential palace in Bishkek protest Kulov's continued detention.**

papers and officially recognized a variety of political parties. International human rights organizations heard comparatively few reports of violations by the Kyrgyz government. Akayev's supporters claimed that he has shown sensitivity to the delicate relations among the country's ethnic groups and has tried to defuse political problems before they arise.

However, other observers considered Akayev's government repressive. A prime example was the prolonged imprisonment of Feliks Kulov, Kyrgyzstan's most prominent opposition leader during Akayev's rule. A former vice president, national security minister, and Bishkek mayor, Kulov at one time was a colleague of President Akayev and considered a strong contender to succeed him. Kulov organized the Ar-Namys opposition party in 1999. The following year, after forcefully criticizing the government, he was arrested and charged with abusing power. He was found innocent, but then in a court proceeding that was closed to the public, the acquittal was reversed and he was handed a seven-year prison term. This sentence was extended in 2002 after he was also found guilty of embezzlement. Kulov was freed during the Tulip Revolution; the country's supreme court later invalidated the charges against him, and today he is the prime minister of Kyrgyzstan.

Kyrgyzstan currently has some 20 active political parties. Widely varied, they range from the Union of Democratic Forces to the Party of Communists of Kyrgyzstan, the Democratic Women's Party of Krygyzstan, and the Party of the Veterans of the War in Afghanistan. The latter represent those who fought during the calamitous Soviet war in Afghanistan during the 1980s.

Kyrgyzstan's government officially permits basic freedom of the press, a policy that stands in contrast with the policies of the former Soviet Union as well as with most of the republics that emerged from the Soviet breakup in 1991. However, there have been complaints that the government does not allow reporters to cover stories about corruption or wrongdoing, and uses its resources to shut down media outlets opposed to the Akayev administration. One international media organization has ranked Kyrgyzstan among the 10 least desirable workplaces for journalists. Reporters have been assaulted, and one who aggressively covered a 1993 government scandal died from his injury.

## Current Government Leaders

Kurmanbek Bakiyev became president of Kyrgyzstan in 2005, taking over when Akayev fled the country in March. Since his election in a landslide in August 2005, his support has waned. There is significant unrest in Kyrgyzstan, as several members of parliament have been shot since tje

**Kyrgyzstan's former prime minister, Nikolay Tanayev (right), is greeted by Turkish prime minister Recep Tayyip Erdogan at a May 2003 meeting in Ankara, Turkey. The prime minister is considered the second-highest official in Kyrgyzstan's government, but 1996 changes to the constitution took some powers from the prime minister and gave them to the president.**

Tulip Revolution. Bakiyev's opponents complain about the use of deadly force in putting prison riots, and allege that the influence of organized crime on the government is increasing.

Bakiyev was born in 1949 in southern Kyrgyzstan. He trained as a Soviet engineer, but soon gained a reputation as a successful factory boss. Throughout the 1990s he developed a career as an economic manager and regional governor. He was appointed prime minister at the end of 2000, but was forced to resign after 2002 the Aksy police shooting. After this, he joined the opposition, and currently heads the People's Movement of Kyrgyzstan.

Felix Kulov, a former Akayev rival, was appointed prime minister of Kyrgyzstan in September 2005. He leads the Ar-Namys (Dignity) party, and comes from northern Kyrgyzstan. He has promised to crack down on corruption and poverty, and said that his partnership with Bakiyev strengthens the country's unity.

# Religion in Kyrgyzstan

Early Kyrgyz and other nomads of the region practiced **shamanism**. They believed selected individuals called shamans had the power to serve as agents between people and the spirit world. Shamans, they believed, could tell them what the spirits wanted them to do, foretell future events, and heal diseases, which people believed were brought on by evil forces. They also engaged in animal worship. They regarded camels, reptiles, owls, and certain other creatures—as well as the sun and various heavenly bodies—as divine objects.

Today, about three-fourths of Kyrgyz are Muslims. However, many ethnic peoples of the region have clung to pagan practices, such as magical rites at certain family and tribal celebrations. Even Islamic observances in the country hint at pre-Islamic customs. There are two Muslim feast days unique to Central Asia: *Kurban ait*, or Day of Remembrance, on June 13, and *Oroz ait* at the end of the holy month of Ramadan.

Most Muslims in Kyrgyzstan belong to the Sunni branch of Islam, the orthodox school followed by more than 80 percent of the world's Islamic population. The most fervent followers of Sunni Islam are found in southwestern Kyrgyzstan, in the Osh oblast.

Islam does not have the overbearing influence in Kyrgyz life or politics that it has in some of the world's other predominantly Muslim countries. After independence, President Akayev vigorously debated with Kyrgyzstan's parliament and succeeded in keeping Islamic requirements out of the country's new constitution. This approach to the constitution was in keeping with Akayev's desire to secure foreign relations on as many sides as he could. While he, like other Central Asian leaders, has sought to strengthen relations with the Muslim Middle East, he has simultaneously sought cooperation with non-Muslim countries. Akayev has suggested, and his policies have shown, that he is much more interested in improving Kyrgyzstan's economy than in shaping a strong Muslim nation.

Islamic practice, as with other religions, was restricted during the Soviet period. Joseph Stalin in particular repressed worship. By 1930, most of the **mosques** across the Soviet Union had been closed, and most of the former **mullahs**, or Muslim worship leaders, no longer served. Many of them, in fact, had been confined to remote labor camps, and some were even executed. During World War II (1939–45), Stalin permitted a temporary revival of religious life because he recognized how the church and mosque could be useful in rallying the Soviet people against Nazi Germany. After the war was ended, however, an agenda of repression policies was resumed. Nikita Khrushchev, premier of the Soviet Union in

**A man enters a mosque in the southern city of Osh. Most of the people of Kyrgyzstan consider themselves Muslims, but few follow the tenets of the religion as strictly as do Muslims in countries like Iran and Saudi Arabia.**

the 1950s and early 1960s, also used a heavy hand in putting down religious worship.

After independence in the 1990s, worship among Central Asians became more common. The majority of Kyrgyz, particularly rural inhabitants, embraced Islam as their ancestors had before the Soviet era. Some 3,000 new mosques were built, largely paid for by Muslim business leaders from Saudi Arabia and other countries. In 1992 Kyrgyzstan was accepted as a member of the Organization of the Islamic Conference (OIC), an association of more than 50 states that promotes economic, social, and political solidarity among Muslim countries.

Akayev and other Central Asian leaders fear Islamic extremists as a political force. During the 1990s, the Akayev government outlawed the Islamic Renaissance Party, which was one of the warring factions involved in neighboring Tajikistan's civil conflict. Kyrgyz officials blame outsiders for the tension brought about by fanatic Muslim groups in the south.

Many of the more recent citizens of the region subscribe to other faiths. Some 20 percent of Kyrgyzstan's citizens are members of the Russian Orthodox Church. Small minorities follow other religions. Non-Muslims live mainly in the northern urban areas, which were more Russified during the tsarist and Soviet periods.

Since independence, an increase in Protestant church membership has been reported in Bishkek and other parts of the north. Officials fear violence will be a result, because radical Muslims regard conversion to other faiths as a punishable offense.

A *manaschï*, or master storyteller, recites the epic of Manas. These traditional performances are often unaccompanied by music.

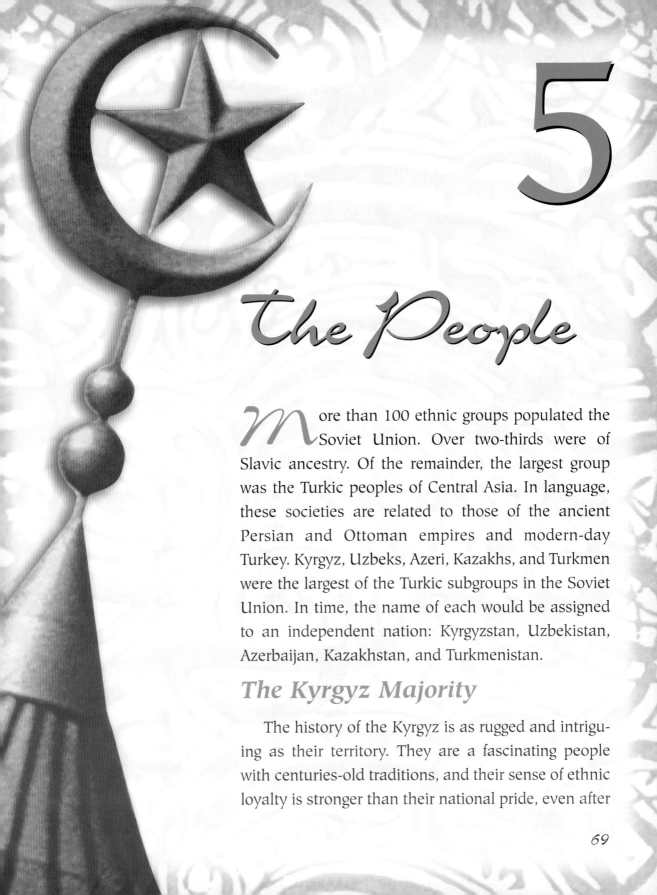

# 5

# the People

More than 100 ethnic groups populated the Soviet Union. Over two-thirds were of Slavic ancestry. Of the remainder, the largest group was the Turkic peoples of Central Asia. In language, these societies are related to those of the ancient Persian and Ottoman empires and modern-day Turkey. Kyrgyz, Uzbeks, Azeri, Kazakhs, and Turkmen were the largest of the Turkic subgroups in the Soviet Union. In time, the name of each would be assigned to an independent nation: Kyrgyzstan, Uzbekistan, Azerbaijan, Kazakhstan, and Turkmenistan.

## The Kyrgyz Majority

The history of the Kyrgyz is as rugged and intriguing as their territory. They are a fascinating people with centuries-old traditions, and their sense of ethnic loyalty is stronger than their national pride, even after decades of enduring enforced loyalty to the state under the Soviets. Some Kyrgyz have left the country and now comprise significant minorities in Uzbekistan, Tajikistan, Kazakhstan, China, Mongolia, and Afghanistan. They rarely marry people of other ethnic backgrounds, but when they do, the foreign partner in the marriage usually becomes Kyrgyz in terms of language and lifestyle.

A Kyrgyz tribe is made up of clans, whose members share a paternal ancestor. The family and its history are central to Kyrgyz society. Young Kyrgyz are taught to respect their parents and grandparents, and are expected to learn the names of everyone in their family for seven generations back. The tribal elders are responsible for keeping genealogical information and passing it along to the new generation.

The nomadic herders of Central Asia have inhabited the steppes and mountains for many centuries. They let their livestock feed in one area until there is nothing left on which to graze, and then move on. Some groups of nomads have wandered long distances, while others have stayed within a smaller area, moving to different pastures with the changing seasons. In the springtime, herders take their livestock up into the mountain meadows for grazing. As summer wanes, they drive them back down into the plains and foothills, and settle in lowland valleys in the winter, during which they can rely on the snow as a source of water.

Through the centuries, the Kyrgyz have raised different kinds of animals. Scholars note that the Kyrgyz primarily raised horses during the 18th and early 19th centuries. This was a period of frequent raiding and warfare, when it was important for a tribe to be able to move quickly. When their lands were annexed to Russia, a time of relative peace followed. The Kyrgyz began raising more sheep, cattle, and camels, and thus were able to better supply the changing demands of the market. Today, they continue to use yaks as beasts of burden for transportation. They also milk the animals, using the milk to make cheese.

One of the things that wanderers of the Central Asian plains have perfected over the centuries is the yurt, a type of mobile dwelling. A framed, tent-like abode variously made of felt, hides, and wool with a carpeted floor, it can be set up and taken down easily and transported from place to place. Yurts are sturdy structures, able to withstand violent wind gusts. Although the dwellings are comparatively small—perhaps the size of a large living room in the United States—as many as 15 individuals can be housed in a single yurt. A majority of Kyrgyz households are large, with several generations of relatives and extended family.

**Kyrgyz horsemen, wearing the armor and bearing the flags of their ancestors, reenact a scene from the Manas epic. Because horses figure prominently in a nomadic culture, horsemanship is a skill that most Kyrgyz learn at a young age.**

**A camp of round, domed yurts, the traditional home of the Kyrgyz.**

Collectivization forced the Kyrgyz to settle in villages, towns, and cities during the Stalin era. As a result, most of Kyrgyzstan's rural herders today have permanent homes in the lowland valleys. But in summer, when they move their stock up into the mountain pastureland, they continue to live in yurts. Even in urban areas, permanent residents put up yurts for weddings and other special occasions.

The yurt is only one of many creations for which the nomadic and seminomadic people of Central Asia are known. Kyrgyz and Kazakh women in particular are famous for their felt making, of which appliqué and mosaic are the most common methods and patterns. Nomads craft intricately carved wooden bowls and other dishware and use animal hides to make flasks and pails.

Several traditions have developed from the Kyrgyz relationship with horses. Rural Kyrgyz learn to ride and tend to the family's horses in early childhood. Until the early 20th century, Kyrgyz cavalrymen engaged in a brutal sport known as *ër soyish*, similar to jousting in medieval Europe. Contestants would try to unseat each other by charging at full speed with blunted pikes. Since ancient times, Kyrgyz and other Central Asian horsemen have practiced **falconry**. Whether using horses for sport or in battle, the Kyrgyz have historically preferred the Mongol breed, which has a reputation for being quick and sturdy.

## Other Ethnic Groups

Kyrgyzstan is by no means a land inhabited only by the Kyrgyz. In fact, it was not until the 1980s that Kyrgyz began to number more than 50 percent of the population in the region that carried their name. About a quarter of the population by that decade was comprised of immigrants of Russian descent. Slavs (Russians and other eastern Europeans) comprised more than half the population of Bishkek (then called Frunze).

Today, more than 80 ethnic backgrounds are represented among Kyrgyzstan's people. Ethnic Kyrgyz comprised about 52 percent of Kyrgyzstan's 2003 population, which is estimated at nearly 5 million people by the CIA World Factbook. Russians and Ukrainians combined for about 20 percent. Most Russians and Ukrainians live in Kyrgyzstan's urban centers of the north. Uzbeks (more than 10 percent of the population), Germans, and Tatars are other sizable population groups. Uzbeks live primarily in southern Kyrgyzstan. Ethnic groups that are smaller in number include the Kazakhs, Dungans, Uighurs, and Tajiks.

Other recent estimates have put the Kyrgyz population of Kyrgyzstan above 60 percent. Kyrgyzstan's population statistics and trends are difficult to determine precisely because of the marked changes that have taken place. Most significant has been the mass exodus of thousands of Russians, Ukrainians, and Germans since the end of the Soviet era. Another factor has been the movement of Kyrgyz, Tajiks, and Uzbeks from one Central Asian country to another, impelled partly by internal upheavals and the tension resulting from Tajikistan's civil war. In time, some of the refugees and migrants have returned to the country they left.

During World War II, Russia fought bitterly against Nazi Germany. Many people of German descent had lived along the Volga River in the Soviet Union since the years before the war. Stalin had them removed and scattered into Siberia and the Central Asian republics. By the time of the Soviet breakup, some 100,000 Germans were living in Kirghizia.

The number of Russian settlers was far greater. Russian settlers began arriving en masse in the late 1800s. During the Stalin era, the Communist government deported many thousands of Russian citizens to the Central Asian republics.

Even before these new settlers arrived in the 20th century, Kirghizia—like other Central Asian territories—was a place of fragmented societies. Its rural people were not united by national borders, and they shared hardly any sense of national pride. Rather, their allegiances lay mainly with their tribes and clans, many of which occupied and roamed lands that overlapped the borders of various Soviet republics. To some extent, Islam provided a common bond between clans, though as with other ethnic traditions, the religion did not foster national unity.

## Departures Since Independence

After independence, many Russians and other minorities were uneasy with the change in power and left Kyrgyzstan. The Russian population in the republic dropped from an estimated 900,000 to 650,000 between 1990 and 1999. Many of the Russians were aware that the native peoples harbored resentment against them for holding some of the best jobs. Also, the Russians had generally kept themselves aloof from Central Asian customs and languages.

Even before the Soviet breakup, the more independent-minded republics were testing Russian dominance over their societies. A 1989 law in

> Although Kyrgyzstan takes its name from the ancient Kyrgyz (Kirghiz) tribal people, their descendants only comprised a minority of the population until the 1980s. Today, the Kyrgyz represent more than 52 percent (some sources estimate more than 60 percent) of the population.

Kyrgyzstan mandated that professional workers and managers—many of them of Russian lineage—master the Kyrgyz language. Other regional republics passed similar language laws. Although these laws were not diligently enforced, they demonstrated a growing resistance to Russian control.

In the early 1990s, a movement in the new government sought to turn all the land in the country over to the Kyrgyz. President Akayev vetoed the measure, decreeing instead that the Kyrgyz people were entitled to half the private land. He also opposed a constitutional proposal that would have allowed only ethnic Kyrgyz to serve as president.

Akayev and other Central Asian leaders understood that their Russian citizens serve important functions in Kyrgyzstan's society. Since the Soviet era, the Central Asian nations have relied largely on Russians as industrial managers and technicians. If all these workers withdrew, they would be difficult to replace. Also, Kyrgyzstan's leaders are aware that a significant percentage of the country's people are neither ethnic Kyrgyz nor Russian. Uzbeks and other citizens oppose "Kyrgyzification" of the country just as they opposed Russification.

## Kyrgyz Society

A significant number of Kyrgyz people dress in western-style clothing, especially in the cities. Some rural Kyrgyz also wear modern clothing, but many still wear traditional garments, including sheepskin coats and leather boots.

School is required for Kyrgyz children aged 7 to 17. Public education is free. The country's impressive literacy rate—approximately 97 percent—proves that high education standards have been preserved from the Soviet era. As in most American public school systems, students attend classes from September through May. After completing the ninth grade, some students enroll in vocational or technical schools, or in pre-college courses. Most higher learning facilities are located in the capital city.

Educators have faced difficult conditions, however. An immediate problem that accompanied independence and the changing of language policies was a scant supply of textbooks. There were few quality books published in the Kyrgyz language, because Soviet educators had used

**A teacher writes her lesson in the Kyrgyz language. Kyrgyzstan's system of public education—a holdover from the Soviet era—has produced a very literate population. Many students learn both their native language as well as Russian, which is also an official language of the country.**

## The People of Kyrgyzstan

**Population:** 5,146,281
**Ethnic groups:** Kyrgyz 65%; Uzbek 14%; Russian 13%;
    Dungan 1%; Ukrainian 1%; Uygur 1%; other, 6%
**Religions:** Muslim 75%; Russian Orthodox 20%; other, 5%
**Age structure:**
    **0–14 years:** 31.6%
    **15–64 years:** 62.3%
    **65 years and older:** 6.2%
**Population growth rate:** 1.29%
**Birth rate:** 22.48 births/1,000 population
**Death rate:** 7.13 deaths/1,000 population
**Infant mortality rate:** 35.64 deaths/1,000 live births
**Life expectancy at birth:**
    **total population:** 68.16 years
    **male:** 64.16 years
    **female:** 72.38 years
**Total fertility rate:** 2.7 children born/woman
**Literacy (age 15 and older who can read and write):**
    99% (1999 est.)

All figures are 2005 estimates unless otherwise noted.
Source: Adapted from CIA World Factbook, 2005.

Russian-language texts. That situation improved in the early 1990s. However, with worsening economic conditions, schools began to fall into disrepair. Energy and funding shortages have resulted in periods without light or heating (a problem in other public buildings, as well). To avoid the expense of constructing new school buildings, many schools operate in shifts as a way to accommodate the growing population. Thousands of teachers, called on to teach two shifts at meager pay, have resigned in response to these demands.

Health care in most parts of the country is deficient. Hospitals generally are less sanitary than in western societies. Medical equipment and drugs are in short supply, and improvements are needed in the medical training field. Heart and lung ailments are the leading causes of death among adults. The country's infant death rate of over 7 percent is high when compared to Russia or to Western countries.

## Men and Women

In most Muslim societies, women are expected to be homemakers, yet Kyrgyzstan stands out as an exception. In order to help their families and tribes to survive, Kyrgyz women have had to perform chores usually reserved for men throughout history. Historical records reveal that some women even led Kyrgyz tribes in warfare.

The role of women has remained constant in the years since independence. Rural women still perform manual labor in much the same ways as men do. In the cities, women—especially those from European backgrounds—have been among Kyrgyzstan's leaders in publishing, banking, and other professions. They have also served in key government roles in a variety of departments, including education, law enforcement, and foreign diplomacy.

## Literature and Arts

Traditional music and dancing are popular in Kyrgyzstan, and performers receive support from the government. Many Kyrgyz performers use traditional instruments, ranging from wooden mouth harps to the *kïyak* and *kobyz*, stringed instruments played with a bow. Certain musical traditions have been carried over from the ancient bards, or minstrels, called **manaschï**. Unaccompanied by musical instruments, these individuals sang ballads glorifying their namesake, Manas, a legendary warrior who defended against invaders from the east. An immense body of lyrics

**Storytelling remains very popular in Kyrgyzstan, and sometimes props and music are used to enhance the performance. Here, a man operates a horse puppet while a woman provides music on the *temir komuz*, or mouth harp. The group is surrounded by appliquéd and embroidered traditional fabrics.**

about Manas has been handed down. Much longer than the *Odyssey*, the classic epic by Homer, *Manas* may be the most extensive epic in world literature. Some *manaschï*, including the noted Kel'dibek of the 19th century, were religious healers who claimed their epic songs could cure the sick. Kyrgyz *manaschï* believed spirits gave them their gifts of poetry and music.

Until the Soviet era, Kyrgyz literature was passed from generation to generation by these minstrels and poets. From childhood, they began committing epic ballads and poems to memory, to be passed on to younger singers. Only as recently as the 20th century was this body of Kyrgyz stories compiled into writings. Togolok Moldo and Toktogul Satylganov were two Kyrgyz intellectuals who led the development of written literature in the early 1900s.

During the Soviet era, artistic expression was restricted in all the republics. For the most part, novels and poetry were written to conform to communist thought. Chingiz Aitmatov is one author and playwright who dared to write about the unhappy climate under Soviet rule. One of his novels, *The Day Lasts More than a Hundred Years*, illustrates Stalin's harshness and the animosity between native cultures and the Russians who settled in the region and assumed control. Another novel, *The Executioner's Block*, was an exposé of corruption. *The White Steamship* sympathized with the traditional customs and values that were increasingly undermined during the 20th century. Despite his critical approach, Aitmatov managed to remain in the good graces of the Soviet authorities.

Ironically, while the Soviets insisted that ethnic groups learn Russian, they allowed the Kyrgyz written language to develop. It combined the three spoken Kyrgyz dialects of different regions of the republic. At first, Kyrgyz was written in Arabic letters, then in Latin and, beginning in the 1940s, in Cyrillic script.

However, by replacing the Arabic alphabets formerly used by Central Asians, the Soviets made it difficult for future generations to study their history and ancient literature. This policy was in keeping with the Soviet agenda of replacing regional traditions and history with propaganda that exclusively extolled the virtues of the communist state. During the Stalin era, the Soviet government even tried to stop ethnic

**A girl strums a three-stringed *komuz*, an instrument that accompanies many traditional Kyrgyz songs.**

peoples from verbally reciting ancient poems about their past heroes.

Karen Dawisha and Bruce Parrott, authors of *Russia and the New States of Eurasia*, explain the effect of the Soviet language policy: "By changing the alphabets of the Central Asian languages to Latin in the 1920s, Moscow made the literatures and publications of many neighboring countries, as well as past writings from Central Asia itself, unintelligible to new generations of Central Asians. The abandonment of the Arabic alphabet eroded Central Asia's waning ties with Persia and diminished its cultural and religious interaction with the Arab world."

Nevertheless, the Soviets made some valuable contributions to the region in fine arts. Thanks to their support, Kyrgyzstan acquired a national philharmonic orchestra as well as a ballet and an opera. The capital of the republic became the home of museums preserving and promoting sculpture, crafts, and other art forms. When the Soviet era ended, however, funding for the arts dwindled. Museums and other artistic institutions fell on hard times. Noted bronze sculptures were stolen from Bishkek's famous sculpture museum, and the impoverished Kyrgyzstani film industry had to look for foreign backing to survive.

## *Food and Drink*

Kyrgyzstan is not known for exotic cuisine. Families of different ethnic backgrounds have their own food traditions, but the basic Kyrgyz diet is simple and practical. It is rooted in centuries of living off the land, and generally consists of meat (typically roast lamb), bread, and products made from milk. Animal parts that are not commonly eaten in western cultures are often cooked with the meat. Horseflesh is frequently eaten and sometimes made into sausage. Potatoes or other vegetables may be included, but vegetables and fruit are not a standard part of Kyrgyz table fare.

A traditional Kyrgyz meal is ***manty***—a dish of large, meat-filled dumplings. Another is ***shurpa***, a soup of vegetables and mutton. *Bes parmak*

**A Kyrgyz family enjoys a meal at their home in the village of Madi. The Kyrgyz diet is simple, comprised mainly of meat, bread, and milk products.**

is a broth or stew meal with mutton and noodles. The term *bes parmak* means "five fingers" because, following Islamic custom, it is eaten with the right hand. Hot tea is a common drink and is typically served plain.

At special feasts, a lamb's head is served whole to the honored guest. This person ritually cuts the eyes and ears into sections and serves them to the others. It is believed that these parts are beneficial to the diners' vision and hearing. The protein-rich meat of the cheek, said to be especially tasty, usually is reserved for elders.

Unlike Muslims in other countries, the people of Kyrgyzstan make little secret of their alcoholic consumption. Many Kyrgyz enjoy vodka and other alcoholic drinks even though Islam forbids alcohol. Kyrgyz and other nomads of the Central Asian mountains and steppes are famous for a milk drink called **kumys**. Known for thousands of years, it is made by churning mares' milk and letting it sour and ferment. Before the rise of Islam, *kumys* was considered a sacred drink by Central Asians. Mongols and other peoples held a spring festival celebrating mares' milk. *Kumys*, which has low levels of alcohol, is brewed in spring and summer—the foaling, or birthing, seasons for mares. Also popular among the Kyrgyz are two other fermented drinks, *bozo* and *shoro*. These are boiled from plants, not milk. Shoro derives from barley, bozo from millet and other grains.

## Problems and Limitations

Sanitation is a serious problem for many of Kyrgyzstan's people. It is not unusual for villages and families to rely on contaminated wells and streams for their drinking water. Much of the nation's public water system needs repair, as do wastewater treatment facilities. Waste metals, chemicals, oils, and sewage from industrial plants and mines have further damaged the environment. Diseases often spread because of these conditions. A related problem has resulted from flawed irrigation systems, which cause a high level of salt content in much of the soil.

The leading social danger is a high crime rate, which stems largely from the narcotics trade. Kyrgyzstan is situated along one of the major routes of drug traffic from Afghanistan to destinations north and west. That has made it easy for drug users in Kyrgyzstan to acquire heroin and other illegal products. Afghanistan is the world's leading producer of narcotics from opium poppies. More than half of these **opiates** are smuggled illegally from Afghanistan over the northern mountains, through Tajikistan and Kyrgyzstan.

Meanwhile, opium poppies and cannabis (marijuana) are cultivated illegally in Kyrgyzstan. Statistics indicate that production of the drugs may have risen in recent years. In 2003, authorities confiscated 3.5 million tons of illegal drugs in Kyrgyzstan—an increase of more than 20 percent from the total seized in 2002.

Officials believe that between 80,000 and 100,000 Kyrgyz use illegal drugs—probably six times the number of users in the country 10 years ago. Leaders are especially worried because opiates such as heroin are hard drugs and are especially dangerous. In the past, most users in Kyrgyzstan only smoked marijuana, which does not cause the same health and social problems as heroin.

Authorities also fear that more and more Kyrgyz are turning to drug dealing because they are trying to overcome personal poverty. More than 90 percent of the nation's drug-related crimes in 2003 involved individuals who were poorly educated and unemployed.

**Drug use is a growing problem in Kyrgyzstan, and the country has received international aid to reduce the number of drug users, as well as to stop the trafficking of heroin out of Central Asia. In this photo, the head of Kyrgyzstan's ministry of Internal Affairs points out the main drug routes from Afghanistan through Kyrgyzstan and neighboring Central Asian countries.**

An estimated 55 percent of Kyrgyzstan's almost 5 million people live below the poverty level. The ***gross domestic product per capita*** in 2002 was $2,900. (Only Tajikistan had a lower income average among the nations of the CIS.) Just more than half the country's workers are farmers and herders; 30 percent is employed in the service sector; the remainder works in small industries.

Kyrgyzstan's communication facilities are underdeveloped. Fewer than 400,000 telephone lines were available in 1997—the most recent year for which data is available—and some 100,000 applicants were waiting for phone service to be installed. Slightly more than a half-million radios and fewer than a quarter-million televisions were in use. The country relies largely on television broadcasts relayed from neighboring republics and from distant Russia and Turkey. In 2001, there were about 52,000 Internet users in Kyrgyzstan, but no local Internet service providers.

One peculiar stumbling block to Kyrgyzstan's ongoing development has been its language changes. During the Soviet era, school was taught in Russian. Few textbooks were available in Kyrgyz when the government made it an official language in 1989. Language difficulties have been especially acute for teachers of scientific and technical subjects. Unlike with Russian, the technical terminology of the Kyrgyz language has not yet evolved with the scientific advances of the 20th century. For example, there are no Kyrgyz words for computer components or telecommunications equipment.

Kyrygz students are also greatly in need of foreign language instruction. Many students in higher education are not fluent in foreign languages, which has posed a handicap for those who wish to study specialized subjects at European, American, and Middle Eastern universities.

A statue of Vladimir Lenin still looms over the main square of Bishkek, the capital of Kyrgyzstan. The country's largest city, Bishkek is both an administrative and cultural center.

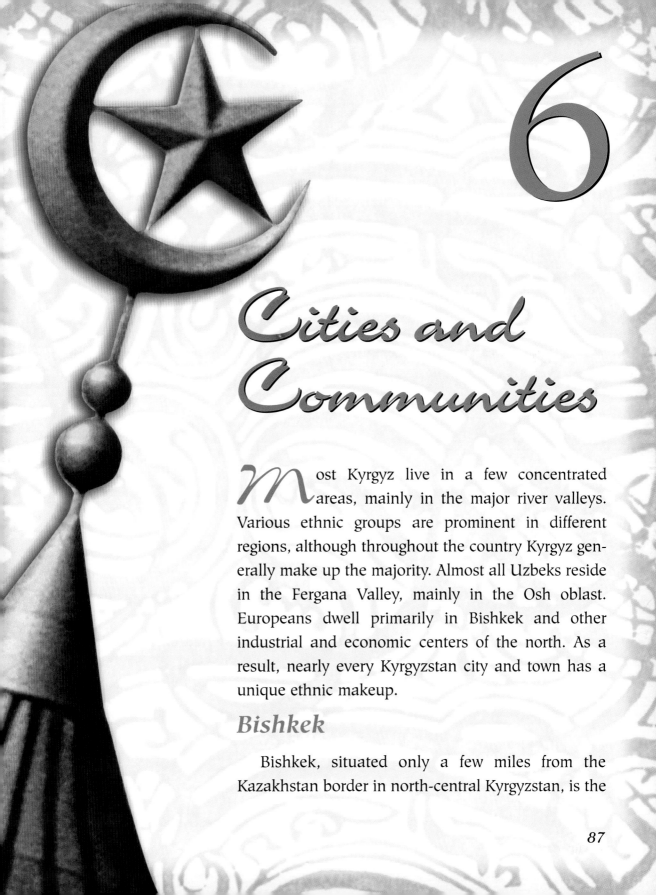

# 6

# Cities and Communities

Most Kyrgyz live in a few concentrated areas, mainly in the major river valleys. Various ethnic groups are prominent in different regions, although throughout the country Kyrgyz generally make up the majority. Almost all Uzbeks reside in the Fergana Valley, mainly in the Osh oblast. Europeans dwell primarily in Bishkek and other industrial and economic centers of the north. As a result, nearly every Kyrgyzstan city and town has a unique ethnic makeup.

## Bishkek

Bishkek, situated only a few miles from the Kazakhstan border in north-central Kyrgyzstan, is the country's capital and the administrative center of the Chuy (or Chui) oblast. (The word *bishkek* refers to a wooden churn used in the making of *kumys*.) It is by far the nation's largest city, with an estimated population of more than 841,000 in 2004. During the Soviet period it was called Frunze and, before that, Pishpek. Bishkek lies in the valley of the Chu River at an altitude of about half a mile—not a great height compared to many of Kyrgyzstan's cities and towns. It lies at a watery crossroads, where the Bolshoy Chuysky Canal intersects the Alamedin and Alaarcha Rivers. Chuy is Kyrgyzstan's most economically stable oblast, with more than 4,000 businesses and industries.

Bishkek was situated along one of the silk trade routes between China and the west. Like many other towns and cities in Kyrgyzstan, Bishkek once was a fortress site. It is believed to have been a sizeable military town as early as the 7th century A.D., but then fell from prominence with the arrival of the Mongols. Kyrgyz nomads found the area to their liking and camped throughout the Chu Valley.

More modern fortifications at Bishkek were developed in 1825 by the Uzbek Khanate of Kokand. During this period, when tax collectors and soldiers took up residence, the nomadic Kyrgyz were repressed while Kokand farmers and merchants thrived.

When Russian forces conquered the fortress in the early 1860s, they renamed it Pishpek. A market and horse-borne mail station were established, and Russian peasants joined ethnic natives in settling the area. Pishpek became the center of government administration for the district in 1878. It soon evolved into a city with European-style streets and squares, in contrast to the narrow, curved streets of other Central Asian cities. By the turn of the century, almost 1,000 Russian-style houses had been built, as well as prominent churches and mosques. The settlers also built schools, hospitals, a movie theater, and a weather station.

Far outstripping the growth of other towns in what is now Kyrgyzstan, Pishpek had some 6,600 residents in 1897 and more than 18,000 by 1913. By this time Russians, Ukrainians, Tatars, and Uzbeks were the main occupants of the central city. Most Kyrgyz—paupers by comparison—lived in yurts outside the city proper, breeding their livestock and tending their crops. Mills and other small industries were established, although rustic bazaars and small shops continued to be the mainstays of Pishpek commerce.

After the Russian Revolution of 1917, Pishpek became the administrative center of a Soviet oblast. In 1926, the oblast became the Kirgiz Autonomous Soviet Socialist Republic, with Pishpek as its capital. That year the city's name was changed to Frunze in honor of a Communist hero, Mikhail Vasilyevich Frunze. General Frunze was the leader of the Red Army, and helped secure Soviet control over Central Asia after the Russian Revolution. When independence came in 1991, the city's name reverted to Bishkek. For the Kyrgyz, the return to the original name was a way for them to revive their ancient heritage, looking back to the centuries before either the tsars or the Soviets dominated them.

Bishkek today is not only the center of Kyrgyzstan's government, but also the national center of culture and economy. Kyrgyz State University and the Academy of Sciences are located in the city, as are other academic institutions. Bazaars bustle with traders and buyers exchanging felt rugs, spices, *kumys*, meats, vegetables, fruits and nuts, and countless other goods. Wide avenues as well as narrow walkways are lined with trees. Irrigation ditches and channels reach through Bishkek. Parks, orchards, museums, theaters, and other features and attractions mark Bishkek as an unrushed but comparatively progressive city.

Along the eastern and western outskirts of Bishkek, farmers grow grains, vegetables, and fruits. There are also food processing and textile factories operating outside the city. Metalworking and the manufacture of agricultural equipment developed in Bishkek during the middle of the 20th century. As a result, today industrial air pollution is a nuisance for residents.

Bishkek enjoys relatively pleasant weather, compared with other Kyrgyzstani towns that sit at higher elevations. Spring frosts end in mid-April, on the average, and more than 300 days of the year bring sunshine (nationwide, the annual average is about 250 sunny days). The months of March through June are the rainiest.

## Osh

Kyrgyzstan's second-largest city is Osh, located in the southwest at the border where Uzbekistan wedges sharply into the Kyrgyzstan's border. The settlement dates to as early as the 9th century A.D. Mongol invaders demolished it during the 1200s, but in time it rose again and became a link in the long east-west trade route that passed through the Fergana Valley.

Osh, the administrative center of an oblast with the same name, has less than half the population of Bishkek. It is an industrial city, producing textiles and processed foods, but it is especially noted as an agricultural market center. Osh oblast contains more than a fourth of Kyrgyzstan's cattle and a fifth of its sheep and goats. Irrigated farms flourish in the outlying valleys, producing grains, cotton, tobacco, citrus fruits, and nuts. Like Bishkek, Osh is something of a cultural and academic center, although on a smaller scale. Osh is home to an international airport, a polytechnic school, and a training college for teachers. It also has a

**Islam is especially influential in the lives of Uzbeks, a prominent ethnic group in the Osh oblast. A shrine found in the city, Takht-i-Suleyman (Solomon's Throne), has long been a pilgrimage destination for the region's Muslims.**

**A young man sells newspapers at a market in Osh, Kyrgyzstan's second-largest city. Although Kyrgyzstan officially permits the press to operate freely, in reality media reports that speak unfavorably of the government have at times been suppressed.**

botanical garden, a museum, a theater, and religious shrines for Muslim inhabitants and visitors.

Along with being a regional center of Islam, Osh also has become a center of the country's illegal drug trafficking since independence. The highway from Osh to Bishkek is a primary route for the transport of drugs from Afghanistan to Europe. The surrounding Fergana Valley, once noted primarily for cotton, silkworm, and fruit production, now is equally known as well for its opium. The ready availability of drugs from within and outside the country, coupled with poor sanitation practices, has created a dangerous scenario. Impoverished drug users share needles, greatly increasing the spread of infectious diseases including AIDS. In 2003, 364 new HIV cases were reported in Kyrgyzstan; health officials traced more than half of them to a prison in the Osh oblast.

## Karakol and Issyk-Kul

Located at the eastern end of Lake Issyk-Kul, Karakol is the main city in eastern Kyrgyzstan and the administrative center of the Issyk-Kul oblast. The Russians established it as a military post after occupying the region in the 1860s. For many years it was named Przhevalsk in honor of Nikolay Przhevalsky, the Russian explorer of the region. Today, Karakol has a museum and theater, as well as a training college for teachers. The city is widely noted for its apple orchards. Besides its location, which makes it an ideal base city for touring Lake Issyk-Kul, Karakol is attractive for its charming, Russian-style cottages. Friendly native families rent sleeping quarters to tourists.

Although Kyrgyzstan is a landlocked country, it has a sizeable port on the western side of Lake Issyk-Kul. The city of Issyk-Kul has a shipyard and is one of Kyrgyzstan's main centers of transportation.

Industries in the Issyk-Kul oblast, mainly established around these two cities, include food processing, the manufacture of building materials, mining operations, cereal processing, and meatpacking. One of the world's largest gold mines is located in this province, at Kumtor.

## Other Cities and Towns

Jalal-Abad, in western Kyrgyzstan, is the country's third-largest city and is the administrative center of the oblast of the same name. The oblast is a major food processing center and the home of various small industries, including coal and gold mining and the manufacture of electric bulbs. Crude oil comes from the province and is refined at a new facility near the city of Jalal-Abad. The city has university branch campuses, a museum, and a theater. Mineral springs in the area inspired the construction of health resorts. Along with its natural treasures, though, Jalal-Abad has seen its share of natural disasters: several thousand residents were rendered homeless after an earthquake shook the region in 1992.

Tokmak, on the Chu River in the north, was established as a fortress in the early 1800s. The river and a railway contributed to industrial growth in the region during the 20th century.

Another city that originated as a trade route fortress is Naryn, located at an elevation of almost 7,000 feet (2,120 meters) on the Naryn River. It guarded the commerce route between the valley of the Chu River in northern Kyrgyzstan and the city of Kashgar in what is now China's Xinjiang (or Sinkiang) province.

Today Naryn is a small industrial city and the administrative seat of the oblast that bears the same name. Though only a fraction of the size of Bishkek, it boasts a theater for performing arts. When fuel shortages in the 1990s curtailed transportation in some of Kyrgyzstan's cities, the leaders in Naryn turned back the pages of time to come up with an interesting alternative: a system of public buses pulled by horses.

Talas, the administrative center of the Talas oblast, is located in a farming district of northwestern Kyrgyzstan. It is renowned for the fine fleece of its sheep. The country's seventh administrative center is Batken in the Batken oblast, which forms the southwestern tip of Kyrgyzstan, bordering Tajikistan and Uzbekistan.

The mountain city of Uzgen lies near the Fergana Valley. Most of its 40,000-plus residents are Uzbek, though some three dozen other cultures make up the rest of the population. The city is believed to have been the site of a fortress approximately 2,000 years ago, as well as a lively trading center on the silk route that

**A farm worker places tobacco leaves on lines to dry at his home in Uzgen, near the Fergana Valley. Most residents of Uzgen are ethnic Uzbeks, rather than Kyrgyz.**

passed through the region. A mausoleum and tower in the middle of the city date to the 12th century. Uzgen is located in a farming area renowned for its red rice, apples, sunflowers, and tobacco. It has a sizable bazaar as well as a university and hospital.

Kyrgyzstan has countless villages. Some were originally Central Asian in character but were strongly influenced by the Europeans during the last century. An interesting example of this cultural mix is found in Leninskoye near Uzgen. Named after the Russian Communist leader, Vladimir Ilyich Lenin, the village of about 2,000 residents lies in winemaking country, surrounded by vineyards. Wine still is produced there, but only by a small number of the original vineyards that remain. Most of the Germans and Russians, who constituted the village majority during the years leading up to independence, left the country in the 1990s. Ethnic Kyrgyz now are the majority, but their neighbors include Uzbek, Tatar, Tajik, Kurd, Uighur, and other ethnic groups. Classes at the village school still are taught in Russian as well as Kyrgyz.

## *Traveling from Place to Place*

Some 11,500 miles (18,500 km) of roads connect the towns and cities, with 260 miles (420 km) of rail lines. The country has two major highways. One highway links Bishkek and Osh. Due to the intervening mountains, it takes about 10 hours to drive between the two cities. (By contrast, it is only a four-hour drive between Bishkek and Almaty, the former capital of neighboring Kazakhstan.)

The other highway extends eastward from Bishkek to Issyk-Kul, then southward to Naryn and, from there, across the mountains into China. Branches of this road fork around the northern and southern sides of Lake Issyk-Kul.

Until the 1920s, the region had only short, narrow railroads used for transporting coal. The Soviets built a rail line from Pishpek (Bishkek) into

**Residents of Bishkek prepare to board a bus. Although highways connect the major cities, most roads in the country are narrow and rough.**

Kazakhstan. There, it connected with the rest of the U.S.S.R.'s rail system. During the mid-1900s, new lines were constructed from the capital to other parts of the republic.

Today the country has more than 60 airports, but only 17 have paved runways. Air travel between northern and southern cities was common until the 1990s, when fuel became expensive and in short supply. To adjust for the lack of fuel, travel simply has become less frequent between the cities, and the north and south have become even more separated. People in southern Kyrgyzstan have bonded more closely with countries of a strong Muslim character, including not just neighboring Uzbekistan but also Afghanistan and Iran. People in the north, meanwhile, have more in common with Kazakhstan and European countries.

A poor communication system has heightened this division between the Bishkek and Osh population centers. Open, easy communication and transportation links help unite different sections of a country. On the other hand, the limited interaction that takes place in Kyrgyzstan at least forces residents to concentrate more on local problems and concerns.

President Akayev lays a wreath at the Tomb of the Unknown Soldier in Warsaw during his visit to Poland in March 2004. As president, Akayev has worked with many foreign leaders to gain assistance for Kyrgyzstan.

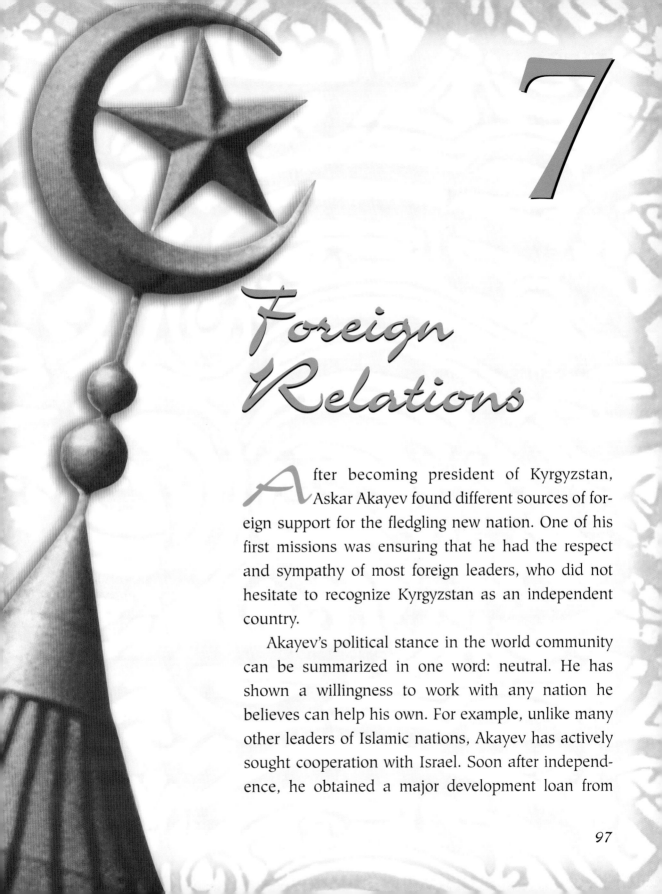

# 7

# Foreign Relations

After becoming president of Kyrgyzstan, Askar Akayev found different sources of foreign support for the fledgling new nation. One of his first missions was ensuring that he had the respect and sympathy of most foreign leaders, who did not hesitate to recognize Kyrgyzstan as an independent country.

Akayev's political stance in the world community can be summarized in one word: neutral. He has shown a willingness to work with any nation he believes can help his own. For example, unlike many other leaders of Islamic nations, Akayev has actively sought cooperation with Israel. Soon after independence, he obtained a major development loan from

Japan, and he visited China to request aid in building hydroelectric plants on the Naryn River.

## Weaving a Wide Web of Relations

Following independence, Kyrgyzstan became a member of the United Nations, World Bank, International Monetary Fund, and other prominent worldwide bodies. In 1998, it became the first CIS member nation in the World Trade Organization. The Kyrgyzstan government has joined other nations in making important environmental agreements. These range from controlling hazardous wastes and air pollution to protecting the earth's ozone layer and other climate concerns.

Over time, Kyrgyzstan developed a complex assortment of foreign relationships. Its two primary import partners are Kazakhstan and Russia. Secondary partners include Uzbekistan, China, the United States, and Germany. In the export sector, Kyrgyzstan sells mainly to Switzerland, Russia, and the United Arab Emirates; secondary export partners include China, Kazakhstan, and Uzbekistan.

While reaching out to the far areas of the globe, Akayev and his government have taken care to maintain ties with the former Soviet republics. With Russia and five other former Soviet republics, Kyrgyzstan signed a security agreement in May 1992. Also, in early 1993 the country was one of seven former republics to sign the CIS charter at a conference in Minsk (the others were Russia, Kazakhstan, Uzbekistan, Tajikistan, Armenia, and Belarus).

What does Kyrgyzstan—a young, poor nation—have to offer foreign countries in exchange for their support? Its value as a trading partner is weak, compared to many other small countries of the world. However, it does have the asset of having a strategically important location. It provides Europeans with an access point into China, and in recent years it has made agreements to set up military bases in the U.S.-led war against terrorists in Central Asia.

## Relations with Regional Neighbors

Some political leaders of the newly independent Central Asian countries have encouraged "pan-Turkism"—increased cooperation among the Turkic peoples of the region. In October 1992, representatives from Kyrgyzstan joined others from Turkey, Kazakhstan, Uzbekistan, Turkmenistan, and Azerbaijan to consider the formation of a Turkic Common Market. The following spring, President Turgut Ozal of Turkey toured the new nations of Central Asia.

Observers believe the countries have too many differences for pan-Turkism to make enough progress, however. They note that the bond of Islam is stronger than inter-ethnic ties in Central Asia, and that animosity already exists among certain ethnic groups in the region. Furthermore, Kyrgyzstan and neighboring countries have significant populations of non-Turkic peoples. Kyrgyz citizens who are originally from Russia, Germany, and elsewhere—or who are descended from European settlers— typically feel closer ties to their familial homelands than to the other nations of Central Asia. Still, governments of the region are working together for the common good whenever necessary. For example, the border disputes between Kazakhstan and Kyrgyzstan, which festered throughout the 1990s, were largely resolved by 2004.

All the former republics have cooperated through the Aral Sea Program. The world's sixth-largest natural lake, the Aral Sea is far to the west of Kyrgyzstan, on the border between Kazakhstan and Uzbekistan. River drainage from Kyrgyzstan, however, has contributed to a major environmental crisis on and around the lake. Irrigation projects in the late 20th century shrunk the lake by an estimated 40 percent, and pollution caused health problems for several million people living in the vicinity. The World Bank and United Nations in 1995 organized a regional conference to develop a plan for remedying the problem. The Aral Sea Program involves

**Kyrgyzstan has been willing to work with its regional neighbors to try to preserve the Aral Sea, which because of irrigation projects has shrunk significantly. This fishing boat was abandoned near Aralsk, Kazakhstan, which was once a major fishing port on the Aral Sea but is now 70 miles (113 km) from the water.**

all five nations of Central Asia which are part of the Aral Sea basin. For its involvement, Kyrgyzstan has constructed a national action plan, designed to control upstream contamination and erosion caused by overgrazing and forest destruction.

## Kyrgyz and Uzbeks

When the Soviet government organized its Central Asian republics during the 20th century, it created boundary lines that were intended to divide some of the larger ethnic groups, thereby preventing a unified resistance to Moscow's control. These borders created territorial disputes among some of the republics. Throughout the Soviet Union and its Eastern European satellite countries, Moscow shifted land in strategic locations from one republic to another. As just one of many examples, Kyrgyzstan long has quarreled with Tajikistan and Uzbekistan over the rich Fergana Valley, which the Soviet government deliberately divided among them.

For years political activists in Uzbekistan have urged their government to reclaim Osh, Kyrgyzstan's second-largest city, along with several smaller towns. Osh, like the rest of southwestern Kyrgyzstan, has a large population of Uzbeks. In 1989, an Uzbek political faction known as Adalat demanded that the Soviet government authorize the annexation of Osh by the Uzbekistan republic. The Kyrgyz living in the oblast put up a strong opposition, and Moscow rejected the Uzbeks' demand. But Kyrgyzstan kept a close eye on Uzbekistan—especially after the president of the neighboring country suggested it was his duty to safeguard the interests of Uzbeks living outside Uzbekistan.

Several hundred people were killed in 1990 during a weeklong clash between Kyrgyz and Uzbek factions, sparked by a land dispute. Kyrgyz from the surrounding mountains attacked Uzbeks in the cities of Osh and Uzgen. Ultimately, Soviet troops were sent in to quell the uprising with brute force.

The Soviet government held such border feuds in check, but after the republics gained independence, the conflicts became a serious matter that

Many Uzbeks who live in southwestern Kyrgyzstan would like to see the city of Osh and other parts of the province annexed to neighboring Uzbekistan. They have the support of some of Uzbekistan's political leaders.

their new governments had to address. Kyrgyzstan's disagreements with Tajikistan and Uzbekistan continued into the 21st century.

At the same time, leaders have worked toward establishing smoother relations. In 1996, Kyrgyzstan signed a friendship treaty with Uzbekistan. The leaders agreed upon dozens of detailed regulations involving relations between the countries, and the two nations, along with Kazakhstan, have established a common economic zone in the Fergana Valley.

## A Balancing Act with World Powers

Since the breakup of the Soviet Union, Central Asian leaders have been too preoccupied with the problems of the present and the future to bemoan the past. However, the people have not forgotten the uncertainties and difficulties they weathered during Soviet domination. During his first term in office, President Akayev finally addressed these feelings of ill will. In 1992, he observed:

> Two hundred and five years ago farsighted representatives of the Kyrgyz nobility sent their ambassadors to St. Petersburg for the first time to come under the protection of the Russian Empire. Our friendship and cooperation date back to that time. . . . Of course there have been bright moments and moments which now give rise to controversy. Nevertheless, something eternal, bright, and kind is characteristic of our mutual relations.

Certain factions within Russia's government would like to see the Soviet Union reconstituted, with the Central Asian states returned to the fold. They consider the former republics a natural part of Russia. One Russian political leader, Vladimir Zhirinovsky, has advocated for the abolition of Kyrgyzstan and the other newly independent states. With a lack of resources, Zhirinovsky argues, these states will ultimately be dependent on Russia, the largest regional power, and the creation of one country would thus simplify matters.

Central Asian leaders have concurred that a measure of reliance on

Russia still is necessary. Soon after independence, Kyrgyzstan signed a cooperation treaty with Russia, and they have since turned to Moscow for guidance in resolving their boundary disputes. Kyrgyzstan also depends on Russia for oil and other resources. The 2001 agreement that made Russian one of Kyrgyzstan's two official languages also made Kyrgyzstan a favored trading partner. Among other things, this means Kyrgyzstan is given priority over other countries in receiving certain vital exports from Russia. The smaller country also has use of international port facilities near St. Petersburg.

**Russia still exerts a great influence on Kyrgyzstan and the other Central Asian republics. In October 2003, Russia opened its first foreign military base since the collapse of the Soviet Union. Here, Akayev (right) shakes hands with Russian president Vladimir Putin at the Russian airbase near Bishkek.**

In December 2002, Kyrgyzstan signed a new security agreement with Russia. Under its terms, some two dozen Russian aircraft and 700 troops were stationed at a Kyrgyz air base. They joined other military forces there from Tajikistan and Kazakhstan. The four countries are CIS members of the new Collective Security Treaty Organization (which also includes Belarus and Armenia). It was formed primarily to counter the spread of Islamic and other terrorist activities, which have threatened governmental stability in Asian and Middle Eastern countries. Some observers see the pact also as a Russian response to growing U.S. influence in Central Asia.

**Kyrgyzstan's minister of defense, General Esen Topoyev (right), discusses security issues with U.S. Secretary of Defense Donald Rumsfeld (left foreground) in the Pentagon, November 2002. Kyrgyzstan supported the United States in its attack on Afghanistan's Taliban government during 2001–02.**

In 1998, Kyrgyzstan became the first member of the Commonwealth of Independent States (CIS) to join the World Trade Organization.

Like other Central Asian countries, Kyrgyzstan has cooperated with the United States in several important areas. The U.S. Secretary of State made the first official visit to Kyrgyzstan early in 1992, and the United States established an embassy in Bishkek shortly afterward. During the 1990s, the two countries signed a number of political and economic agreements, and the United States contributed more than $300 million to humanitarian and economic relief in Kyrgyzstan. Japan, Switzerland, France, Canada, and other countries also have contributed significant monetary aid, and the European Community has sent technical specialists to help manage economic matters.

In the aftermath of the September 2001 terrorist attacks in New York and Washington, D.C., the United States launched an antiterrorist campaign in Afghanistan. Because of its nearness (only Tajikistan lies between Afghanistan and Kyrgyzstan), the United States wished to use an air base in Kyrgyzstan for some of its Afghan military operations and sought President Akayev's permission, which he granted.

The United States has been helping the Kyrgyzstan government in its fight against illegal drugs. In 2003, more than $6 million was allocated to help Kyrgyzstan develop a Drug Control Agency. Because terrorists are known to generate operating income through drug trafficking, drug enforcement is pivotal in combating worldwide terrorism.

International narcotics trafficking in Kyrgyzstan has attracted the attention of other governments as well. China has shown concern because drug money may be supporting separatist militants in Xinjiang, the Chinese province that shares Kyrgyzstan's long, mountainous southeastern border.

European Union officials visiting Central Asia in early 2004 also made the fight against narcotics part of their agenda. Europe is a prime destination of illicit drugs from Afghanistan and other Asian countries.

At independence, Kyrgyzstan faced a series of mountain boundary disputes with China. But President Akayev worked for closer relations with the larger power. In 1998, the two countries signed a friendship agreement and China promised to invest some $8 million in Kyrgyzstani factory operations; in 2000, Kyrgyzstan ceded more than 463 square miles (1,200 sq km) of disputed territory to China.

## Kyrgyzstan and the Islamic World

The 1978–79 revolution in Iran brought Islam to the attention of millions of people around the world—many for the first time. For those who knew little or nothing of Islam, it was a shocking introduction. Shiite fundamentalists, united behind an exiled religious scholar named Ayatollah Ruholla Khomeini, brought down the pro-U.S. government of the Iranian shah. Many Americans had considered the shah's regime to be one of the world's strongest and a close ally of the United States. The shah's regime was replaced by an Islamic leadership that demanded strict obedience to Shiite teachings. Ruling clerics seized total control by wiping out and forbidding all political opposition. Anyone accused of criticizing the revolutionary government was imprisoned or otherwise removed. Iranians—most of whom had supported the revolution in hopes it would improve the lives of common people—found themselves living in fear.

Some outside observers became afraid, too. They feared the ayatollah's political, militant brand of Islam would catch fire among Muslims in other nations and bring chaos to the world order. Iran bordered the Soviet republic of Turkmenistan, one of the five Central Asian republics. Naturally, when the Soviet Union dissolved, experts were concerned that

**Kyrgyzstan is a member of the Shanghai Cooperation Organization (SCO), a strategic economic partnership that also includes China, Russia, Tajikistan, Kazakhstan, and Uzbekistan. Here the countries' representatives celebrate the opening of a new SCO office.**

the predominantly Muslim populations of inner Asia might embrace Islamic fundamentalism.

While no major revolution has taken place, radical Islamic groups have caused alarm. Armed Muslims in 1999 invaded the Batken province, the southwestern finger of Kyrgyzstan that juts between Tajikistan and Uzbekistan. Two people were killed and several hostages, including visiting scientists from Japan, were held for two months. The attackers' stated objective was to make the Fergana Valley a separate Muslim state.

Deeper, older issues distract Central Asians from allying themselves too closely under the Muslim banner. The people are more firmly bonded by their various tribal and national backgrounds, a fact that Kyrgyzstan's leaders heeded in shaping the new constitution and in forging relations with Muslim states. Although Islam is the majority faith, Kyrgyzstan's leaders have tried not to alienate others.

One writer on Central Asian affairs, Boris Z. Rumer, has pointed out the balancing act that the regional governments must manage between Islamic and Russian alliances:

> The leaders of Central Asian states are seeking to obtain as much economic aid from the Middle East as they can, while at the same time professing their desire to maintain their ties with Russia. The reason is clear. The Central Asian leaders need Moscow for defense, but Muslim capital for development. Consequently, to use a Russian peasant saying, they are trying to milk two cows at the same time.

Three Islamic nations in particular—Iran, Turkey, and Saudi Arabia—made special efforts to cultivate ties with the Central Asian countries after the breakup of the U.S.S.R. Even though an Iranian-style revolution seems unlikely, some westerners worry that Islam's influence in the developing countries may go beyond economic cooperation. They fear Islamic fundamentalism in Central Asian politics, and are also concerned about Islamic terrorist groups operating from remote Central Asian bases.

## An Uncertain Future

Kyrgyzstan is a land of rugged but awesomely beautiful mountains, steppes, and valleys. If a tourism industry can be developed, Kyrgyzstan may become a popular destination for foreigners. Of the five former republics of Central Asia, Kyrgyzstan is perhaps the most open and receptive to tourists. Its government recognizes that tourism has a potential comparable to that of foreign investment.

However, before this can happen, the unrest and corruption in the country must be addressed. Despite the euphoria of the 2005 Tulip

Revolution, Kyrgyzstan remains a poor nation with many problems. As it pushes into the 21st century, its challenges are to resolve its ethnic tensions, provide a peaceful and stable society, and create a strong economy despite its limited trade resources. Observers believe its economic health—and hence its general prosperity—will depend on its ability to attract international investors and improve its industries.

| | |
|---|---|
| **ca. 500 B.C.–A.D. 500:** | A warrior people known as the Scythians settle and live in the region that is now Kyrgyzstan. |
| **1st century B.C.:** | Trade between China and the West begins with the formation of silk routes through Central Asia. |
| **ca. A.D. 570:** | Muhammad, the founder of Islam, is born. |
| **9th century:** | Islam begins to spread into Central Asia. |
| **ca. 10th century:** | Kyrgyz begin migrating into Tian Shan Mountains. |
| **Early 13th century:** | The Mongols subdue Central Asia. |
| **1700s:** | The Kokand Khanate of the Uzbeks begins to control part of Central Asia including Kyrgyzstan. |
| **1876:** | Russia defeats the Kokand Khanate; Kyrgyzstan becomes part of Russia's Central Asian colony. |
| **1916:** | Kyrgyz join other ethnic groups in a tragic, unsuccessful uprising against Russian rule. |
| **1917:** | The Russian Revolution ends the era of the tsars. |
| **1922:** | The Union of Soviet Socialist Republics (U.S.S.R.) is established in what was formerly tsarist Russia. |
| **1925:** | Kirghizia is named an autonomous oblast of the U.S.S.R. |
| **1930s:** | Soviet leader Joseph Stalin forces nomadic tribes of the Central Asian republics onto state-owned farms through the program of collectivization. |
| **1936:** | Kirghizia attains the status of a full republic. |
| **1980s:** | Support for the Communist system continues to decline throughout the Soviet republics. |

# Chronology

| | |
|---|---|
| **1990:** | Askar Akayev is chosen president of the Kirghiz Soviet Socialist Republic, which changes its name to Kyrgyzstan; several hundred people are killed during a clash between Kyrgyz and Uzbek factions. |
| **1991:** | Kyrgyzstan becomes an independent republic; the Soviet Union dissolves; Akayev is elected to the presidency by popular vote. |
| **1992:** | Kyrgyzstan becomes a member of the United Nations and the International Monetary Fund. |
| **1993:** | Kyrgyzstan adopts constitution; joins neighboring Kazakhstan and Uzbekistan in forming the Central Asian Economic Union. |
| **1996:** | Kyrgyzstan enters an agreement to strengthen ties with Kazakhstan, Russia, and Belarus. |
| **1998:** | Kyrgyzstan signs a friendship declaration with China. |
| **2002:** | Five Uzbek demonstrators are killed by police in southwestern Kyrgyzstan. |
| **2003:** | Voters approve a constitutional referendum that gives the president greater authority. |
| **2004:** | In April, opponents of Nikolay Tanayev come within three votes of ousting the prime minister in a parliamentary vote of confidence. |
| **2005:** | Irregularities in parliamentary elections lead to a series of nationwide protests in March. The "Tulip Revolution" causes Akayev to flee the country; he resigns as president in April. In July former prime minister Kurmanbek Bakiyev is elected president. |
| **2006:** | The Bakiyev administration continues to struggle against allegations of corruption. |

Glossary

**alpine**—typical of or found in high mountains.

**arable**—suitable for farming.

**collectivization**—to organize in a system marked by collective, or group, control over the means of production and distribution.

**cosmopolitan**—sophisticated.

**falconry**—hunting with birds of prey.

**gross domestic product per capita**—the total value of all goods and services produced domestically in a year, divided by midyear population.

**irrigation**—the act of supplying water to a region of land through artificial means.

**khanate**—an administrative region governed by a Mongolian or Turkic khan.

*kumys*—a milk beverage of the Central Asian mountains.

*manaschï*—a nomadic Kyrgyz minstrel.

*manty*—meaty dumplings, popular in Kyrgyzstan.

**mosque**—a Muslim place of worship.

**mullah**—a Muslim religious leader.

**nomadic**—characteristic of a group of people who continually move in search of pasture for their herds or food and water.

**oblast**—a governmental province in the former Soviet Union, or a governmental division in present-day Kyrgyzstan.

**opiates**—drug products derived from opium poppies.

**shamanism**—the religious practice of ancient Central Asian nomads.

*shurpa*—a soup typically made with lamb and vegetables.

**steppes**—broad, stark areas covered by short grass; these have been long used by nomadic peoples for grazing their livestock.

**yurt**—collapsible, tent-like dwelling of Central Asian nomads.

# Further Reading

Alaolmolki, Nozar. *Life After the Soviet Union: The Newly Independent Republics of Transcaucasus and Central Asia*. Albany: State University of New York Press, 2001.

Barbour, William, and Carol Wekesser, eds. *The Breakup of the Soviet Union*. San Diego: Greenhaven Press, 1994.

Curtis, Glenn E., ed. *Kazakhstan, Kyrgyzstan, Tajikistan, Turkmenistan, and Uzbekistan: Country Studies*. Washington, D.C.: Library of Congress, 1997.

Dawisha, Karen, and Bruce Parrott. *Russia and the New States of Eurasia*. Cambridge, U.K.: Cambridge University Press, 1994.

Kort, Michael G. *The Handbook of the Former Soviet Union*. Brookfield, Conn.: Millbrook Press, 1997.

Maclean, Fitzroy. *All the Russias*. New York: Smithmark Publishers, 1992.

Meyer, Karl E. *The Dust of Empire: The Race for Mastery in the Asian Heartland*. New York: Perseus Publishing, 2003.

Pryce-Jones, David. *The Strange Death of the Soviet Empire*. New York: St. Martin's Press, 1995.

Thubron, Colin. *The Lost Heart of Asia*. New York: HarperCollins Publishers, 2000.

Vassiliev, Alexei, ed. *Central Asia: Political and Economic Challenges in the Post-Soviet Era*. London: Saqi Books, 2001.

**http://www.kyrgyzstan.org**

Website of the Embassy of Kyrgyzstan in Washington, D.C.

**http://www.cia.gov/cia/publications/factbook/geos/kg.html**

Current country statistics and general information about Kyrgyzstan are available at the CIA World Factbook.

**http://eng.gateway.kg**

A website of the Development Gateway Foundation, a group that sets up information systems in developing countries. The site contains information about Kyrgyzstan's government, economics, history, society, and geography.

**http://www.eurasianet.org/resource/kyrgyzstan/index.shtml**

Website containing links to news about Kyrgyzstan, as well as political, social, economic, cultural, and environmental content. It is operated by the Central Eurasia Project of the Open Society Institute, based in New York.

**http://www.freenet.kg/db**

A Kyrgyz site that contains Central Asian news items as well as background information about the country.

**http://www.lonelyplanet.com/destinations/central_asia/kyrgyzstan**

Kyrgyzstan's page on the online travel guide site of Lonely Planet, an independent travel publisher.

# Index

Academy of Sciences, 89
Adalat, 101
 *See also* Uzbek (ethnic group)
Afghanistan, 70, 83, 105
agriculture, 27, 51–55, 70–72, *104*
 *See also* economy
AIDS, 91
 *See also* social problems
Aitmatov, Chingiz, 79–80
Akayev, Askar, 18–19, 45–47, *50*, 63–64,
 67, 75, *96*, 108–109
  and the economy, 57
  and foreign relations, 64–66, *96*,
   97–98, 102–106
  human rights record of, 60–63
Akayeva, Mayram, *19*
Aksy, *48*, 49
Alai mountain range, 22
Alamedin River, 87–88
Alma-Ata, 94–95
Aral Sea, 23–24
Aral Sea Program, 99–100
 *See also* foreign relations
arts and literature, 78–81
Assembly of People's Representatives,
 59–61
 *See also* government
At-Bashy mountain range, 22
Azeri (ethnic group), 69

Bakiyev, Kurmanbek, 49, 60, 63–64
banking, 55–56
Batken, 92–93
Batu Khan, 37
Beknazarov, Azimbek, 47–48
Bishkek, 14, 30, 40, 58–59, *86*, 88–89,
 94–95
  population, 73, 86
Bolshevik Revolution of 1917, 16–17,
 40–43, 89
Bolshoy Chuysky Canal, 88

border disputes, 99, 100–101
 *See also* ethnic groups
Britain, 57

Central Asian uprising (1916), 40–41
Chatkal Mountains, 22
Chatyr-Kol (Lake), 24
China, 16, 57, 70, 98, 105–106
Chu River, 24, 92–93
Chu Valley, 27, 30
Chuy oblast, 88
cities, 38, 86–96
climate, 28, 89–90
Collective Security Treaty Organization,
 104
collectivization, 44, 52, 72
 *See also* agriculture
Commonwealth of Independent States
 (CIS), 46, *47*, 60, 98, 104
communications infrastructure, 85, 95
communism, 18, 40–46, 60

Dawisha, Karen, 81
d'Encausse, Hélène Carrère, 40
Drug Control Agency, 105
drugs, 27, 83–84, 90–91, 104–106
 *See also* social problems
Dungan (ethnic group), 73

economy, 19, 46–47, 51–59
education, 75–77, 85
elections, 47–49, *50*, 60–61, 63–64
 *See also* government
environmental problems, 24, 28–31,
 52–53
Erdogan, Recep Tayyip, *64*
ethnic groups
Kyrgyz, *12*, 13–15, *25*, 26, 30, *32*, 35,
 37–41, 43, 52, 58, 61, 64–66, 69–73,
 78–85, 87–89, 94, 100–102
  number of, 69

Numbers in **bold italic** refer to captions.

tension between, 26, 45, 59, 67, 74, 100–102, 109
Uzbek, 26, 39, 40, 45, 59, 63, 69, 73, 87, 88, 89, 90, **93**, 94, 100–102

family life, 70–71, 78
Fergana Valley, 22, 24, **25**, 26–27, **29**, 30, 87, 90–91, **93**, 101, 102, 107
flag, 13, 15, **60**
food and drink, 81–83
foreign investment, 57–58, 108
    *See also* economy
foreign relations, 57–58. 97–109
Frunze. *See* Bishkek
Frunze, Mikhail Vasilyevich, 89
Frye, Richard N., 34

gender roles, 78
Genghis Khan, 36–37
geographic features, **20**, 21–31
Germany, 41, 57, 66, 74, 98, 99
glaciers, 22–23, 58
Golden Horde, 37, 39
    *See also* Mongol empire
Gorbachev, Mikhail, 45
government, 59–64

health care, 44, 53, 78
*The Heritage of Central Asia* (Frye), 34
history
    independence, 45–49
    Mongol empire, 36–38
    under Russia, 39–40
    Silk Road trade, 34–35
    under the Soviet Union, 40–45
    spread of Islam, 38
Hulegü Khan, 38
human rights, 61–63
hydroelectric power, 25, 29, 55, 57, 98

independence, 45–46, 53, 54, 55–56, 61, 63, 66, 74–75, 97–98
industry, 54, 57

*See also* economy
"inner Asia," 15
International Monetary Fund (IMF), 57, 98
Iran, 16, 18, 95, 106, 108
Islam, 18, 30, 45, 65–67, 74, 82–83, 91
    militant, 18, 47, 67, 104, 106–108
    spread of, 18, 38
    *See also* religion
Issyk-Kul, 91, 92
Issyk-Kul (Lake), **22**, 23–24, 33, 55, 59, 91, 92

Jalal-Abad, **48**, 92

Kalmyk (ethnic group), 39
Kara Khitai, 35
Karakol, 90–91
Kazakh (ethnic group), 40, 69, 72, 73
Kazakhstan, 16, 23, 24, 26, 28, 30, 35, 39, 45, 55, 56, 69, 70, 87, 94–95, 98, 99, **100**, 102, 104, **107**
Kel'dibek, 79
    *See also* Manas
Khan-Tengri, 23
Khomeini, Ayatollah Ruholla, 106
Khrushchev, Nikita, 66
Kirghiz Autonomous Oblast, 42–43
Kirghizia. *See* Kyrgyzstan
Kok Shaal-Tau mountain range, 22
Kulov, Feliks, **62,** 63, 64
Kumtor, 92
Kurban ait, 65
    *See also* Islam
Kyrgyz (ethnic group), 16–17, 26, **32**, 45–46, 69–76, 87, 100–102
    history of the, 36–38, 39–43, 69
    traditions of the, 70–73, 74–76
Kyrgyz Republic. *See* Kyrgyzstan
Kyrgyz State University, 89
Kyrgyzstan
    the arts, 78–81
    cities, 38, 86–96

# Index

climate, 28, 89–90
economy, 19, 46–47, 51–59
education, 75–77, 85
foreign relations, 57–58, 97–109
geographic features, *20*, 21–31
government, 59–64
health care, 44, 53, 78
history, 33–49
independence, 45–46, 53, 54, 55–56
location and area, 15–16, 21–22, 26–27
population, 17, 28, 30, 40, 58, 69–75, 77
under Russia, 39–42
social problems, 28–31, 83–85, 91
under the Soviet Union, 14, 16–18, 40–45, 46, *47*, 51, 52, *57*, 60–61, 69, 74, 76, 80, 85, 100–101, 102, *103*

Lake Issyk-Kul. *See* Issyk-Kul (Lake)
languages, 18–19, 39, 43, 45, 69–70, 74, 75–78, 81, 85
legal system, 59
*See also* government
Legislative Assembly, 59
*See also* government
Lenin, Valdimir, 41, *42*, *86*, 94
Leninskoye, 94
literacy rate, 76, 77
*The Lost Heart of Asia* (Thubron), 56

Maili Suu River, *29*
Manas, *12*, 13–14, 43, *68*, *71*, 78–79
Manchu (ethnic group), 39
Marx, Karl, 41
military, 59–60
*See also* government
mining, 55
*See also* economy
Moldo, Togolok, 79
Mongol empire, 35–39, 55, 88, 90
*See also* history
Muhammad, 38
*See also* Islam

Naryn, 93, 94
Naryn River, 24, *25*, 29, 55, *57*, 93, 98
Nicholas II (Tsar), 41
*See also* Russia
nomadic lifestyle, 14, 27, 33, 34–35, 37–38, 52, 70, *71*, 73
*See also* Kyrgyz (ethnic group)

oblasts, 42, 43, 47, 52, 59
*See also* government
oil, 27, 92
Organization of the Islamic Conference (OIC), 67
*See also* Islam
Oroz ait, 65
*See also* Islam
Osh, 21, 30, 45, 65, *66*, 87, 90–91, 94, 95, 101
Ozal, Turgut, 99

pan-Turkism, 99
*See also* foreign relations
Parrott, Bruce, 81
Pik Pobedy (Mount Victory), 23
Pishpek. *See* Bishkek
political parties, 43–44, 60–62, 67
*See also* government
population, 17, 28, 30, 40, 58, 69–75, 77
poverty, 84
*See also* social problems
Przhevalsk. *See* Karakol
Przhevalsky, Nikolay, 24, 92
Putin, Vladimir, *103*

religion, 64–67
*See also* Islam
Rumer, Boris Z., 108
Rumsfeld, Donald, *104*
Russia, 15–19, 30, 35, 37, 39–42, 58, 70, 74, 78, 85, 98, 102–104, 108
*See also* Soviet Union
*Russia and the New States of Eurasia* (Dawisha and Parrott), 81

Russian Turkistan, 39

Saki tribal people, 33
Satylganov, Toktogul, 79
Scythians, 33
    *See also* history
shamanism, 64–65
    *See also* religion
Shanghai Cooperation Organization
    (SCO), *107*
Silk Road, 27, 34–35
social problems, 28–31, 83–85, 91
    *See also* drugs
som (currency), 56
Song-Kul (Lake), 24
Soviet Union, 14, 16–18, 40–45, 46, *47*,
    51, 52, *57*, 60–61, 69, 74, 76, 80, 85,
    100–101, 102, *103*
        and religion, 65–66
        *See also* Russia
Stalin, Joseph, *42*, 44, 52, 65–66, 72, 74,
    80
stele, *32*
Stewart, Desmond, 38

Tajik (ethnic group), 16, 73, 94
Tajikistan, 16, 26, 28, 35, 51, 58, 67, 70,
    74, 83, 85, 93, 98, 101–102, 104, 105,
    *107*
Takht-i-Suleyman, 90
Talas, 51, 93
Talas Valley, 27
Tanayev, Nikolay, 63, *64*
Temujin. *See* Genghis Khan
terrorism, 18, 98, 104, 105, 108
the Thirty, 43, 44
Thubron, Colin, 56
Tian Shan Mountains, *20*, 22–24, 27, 30,
    35

Tokmak, *20*, 92
Topoyev, Esen, *104*
tourism, 24, 58–59, 92, 108
    *See also* economy
trade, 27, 34–35, 37, 38
    *See also* history
transportation, 18, 30, 59, 92, 95
Tulip Revolution, 49, 50, 60, 63, 64, 108
Turkey, 57, *64*, 69, 85, 99, 108
Turkmen (ethnic group), 69
Turkmenistan, 16, 69, 99, 107

Uch-Korgon, *17*
Uighurs (ethnic group), 73, 94
United Nations, 98, 99
United Soviet Socialist Republics
    (U.S.S.R.). *See* Soviet Union
United States, 57, 71, 98, *104*, 105–106
Usun tribal people, 33
Uzbek (ethnic group), 26, 39, 40, 45, 59,
    63, 69, 73, 87, 88, 89, 90, *93*, 94,
    100–102
Uzbekistan, 16, 24, 26, 28, 30, 56, 69, 70,
    90, 93, 95, 98, 99, 101–102, *107*
Uzgen, 93–94, 101

wildlife, 23
World Bank, 98, 99
World Trade Organization, 46, 98, 105
World War I, 40
World War II, *17*, 66, 74
Wu Ti, 27

Yenisey River, 37
yurt, 13, *14*, *41*, 58, *60*, 71, *72*, 89

Zhirinovsky, Vladimir, 102

# Picture Credits

The **Foreign Policy Research Institute (FPRI)** served as editorial consultants for the Growth and Influence of Islam in the Nations of Asia and Central Asia series. FPRI is one of the nation's oldest "think tanks." The Institute's Middle East Program focuses on Gulf security, monitors the Arab-Israeli peace process, and sponsors an annual conference for teachers on the Middle East, plus periodic briefings on key developments in the region.

Among the FPRI's trustees is a former Secretary of State and a former Secretary of the Navy (and among the FPRI's former trustees and interns, two current Undersecretaries of Defense), not to mention two university presidents emeritus, a foundation president, and several active or retired corporate CEOs.

The scholars of FPRI include a former aide to three U.S. Secretaries of State, a Pulitzer Prize–winning historian, a former president of Swarthmore College and a Bancroft Prize–winning historian, and two former staff members of the National Security Council. And the FPRI counts among its extended network of scholars—especially its Inter-University Study Groups—representatives of diverse disciplines, including political science, history, economics, law, management, religion, sociology, and psychology.

**Dr. Harvey Sicherman** is president and director of the Foreign Policy Research Institute in Philadelphia, Pennsylvania. He has extensive experience in writing, research, and analysis of U.S. foreign and national security policy, both in government and out. He served as Special Assistant to Secretary of State Alexander M. Haig Jr. and as a member of the Policy Planning Staff of Secretary of State James A. Baker III. Dr. Sicherman was also a consultant to Secretary of the Navy John F. Lehman Jr. (1982–1987) and Secretary of State George Shultz (1988).

A graduate of the University of Scranton (B.S., History, 1966), Dr. Sicherman earned his Ph.D. at the University of Pennsylvania (Political Science, 1971), where he received a Salvatori Fellowship. He is author or editor of numerous books and articles, including *America the Vulnerable: Our Military Problems and How to Fix Them* (FPRI, 2002) and *Palestinian Autonomy, Self-Government and Peace* (Westview Press, 1993). He edits *Peacefacts*, an FPRI bulletin that monitors the Arab-Israeli peace process.

**Daniel E. Harmon** is an author and editor in Spartanburg, South Carolina. He has written more than 40 nonfiction books, a mystery short story collection, and numerous magazine and newspaper articles. Harmon has served for many years as associate editor of *Sandlapper: The Magazine of South Carolina* and editor of *The Lawyer's PC*, a national computer newsletter published by West. His special interests include nautical history and the traditional music of different countries and cultures.